To Jo

Hoping this
made jono

Love,
Mum.

HOW TO DEVELOP YOUR GIFT

A Practical Guide To Enhancing And Discovering Your Gift

Contents:

Chapter 1 The first leg of my journey. **Page 14**

Chapter 2 Deciding what to do in life. **Page 18**

Chapter 3 Teach yourself intuitively from within. **Page 22**

Chapter 4 Your inspiration starts with the visual. **Page 26**

Chapter 5 Your own heart is where your uniqueness lies. **Page 30**

Chapter 6 Failure what's that. **Page 34**

Chapter 7 Creating a gift that people seek out. **Page 38**

Chapter 8 Keep your eye on the goal. **Page 42**

Chapter 9 Always be proactive. **Page 46**

Chapter 10 Be extraordinary. **Page 48**

Chapter 11 The power of visualisation. **Page 50**

Chapter 12 Choose being creative over being rigid. **Page 54**

Chapter 13 Move with the times. **Page 56**

Chapter 14 Modern contentment verses old fashioned contentment **Page 60**

Chapter 15 The magician's hat. **Page 64**

Chapter 16 The art of sky gazing. **Page 70**

Chapter 17 Points of a compass. **Page 74**

Chapter 18 Creating effective prompts. **Page 78**

Chapter 19 What to do if you have your gift . **Page 82**

Chapter 20 Copying is creative if done in a unique way. **Page 84**

Chapter 21 Seeing creativity as a science. **Page 88**

Chapter 22 The culture of gift giving. **Page 92**

Chapter 23 Rachael's dream verse's the American Dream. **Page 96**

Chapter 24 Discerning the difference. **Page 100**

Chapter 25 Art is about inspiring change, too. **Page 104**

Chapter 26 Write your own book. **Page 106**

Chapter 27 The cleverness behind your uniqueness. **Page 110**

Chapter 28 The importance of joy. **Page 112**

Chapter 29 The edges of the box. **Page 114**

Chapter 30 Managing conflict and the loss of ideas. **Page 116**

Chapter 31 Know what your worth is. **Page 120**

Chapter 32 Create your own destiny. **Page 122**

Chapter 33 Refining and defining. **Page 124**

Page 128 Artwork and Social Media details

Page 166 Acknowledgements

Page 168 Artwork/Illustration Acknowledgements

About the Author

Rachael is a practicing artist who currently explores her drawing technique through the medium of fashion illustration.

She has always had a talent for writing, and has written a lot for creative reasons.

This book came to her through inspiration as she wanted to help people who are struggling to find and develop their gift as well as help those who are more established in there gift area find new insights to enhance their life. She is currently working on a sequel to this work.

How to Develop your Gift .

Preface: When I wrote this book I wanted to create a book like 'Ways Of Seeing' By John Berger, but with the intention of showing people how to create groundbreaking pieces of work. I wrote this book, so I can teach you in an afternoon how to change your life. It is a practical book and you will need to do the work to get results. I hope, this book will, move you on to greater heights so you become a successful artist or producer of your gift in your own right. You can also view my work that I created as a result of this study at, www.facebook.com/fashionillustrationmagazine .

ENJOY YOUR GIFT

INTRODUCTION:

THE PURPOSE OF THIS BOOK IS TO INSPIRE, AND TO HOPEFULLY CREATE A TRIBE OF LIKE MINDED PEOPLE WHO ARE ON A CREATIVE MISSION. It is also about people taking creative gift action and coming back to the tribe to share. It's about sharing my original views on creative self discovery, and it is about leadership. It is more about how you can be a leader of your own life, creatively, and it gives you valuable tips on how to do this. We are no longer sheep and you are also not a leader of sheep. You are a leader, who when prepared shares with your fellow tribe members the wide open spaces that you have discovered, for the purpose of them also finding this wide open space too, and so on, and so on, so that the cycle continues. As this cycle further continues, we can try to further unravel the creative control the system has on us, and our talents. It's about unlearning sheep behaviour towards our education, our talent, and our lives, and it is most importantly about 'How to Develop Your Gift'.

I hope this book offers a solution, a much needed solution, on how we are going to build our own enterprises, and take back creative control of our lives. This book isn't about changing the educational system. It just seeks to make it wobble a bit from side to side, just to create a new awareness. The education system evolved as it stands today around the time of the industrial revolution, so it is a product of that. But the business model that supported the industrial revolution and the educational system has changed, and so therefore, so must we. This book shows you how.

This book is also for people who want more out of their career, but can't afford to get fired, or change their careers at the moment. This book gives you practical and well researched options and an alternative to living in the rat race that you are never going to win anyway. This book teaches you how to focus on your own sovereignty, and it will help you lift your head high, even if it's just so you can look kindly down upon the people who never believed in your dream. This book teaches you that you can have your dream, and gives you well researched ideas on how to achieve it. You may though, have your own methods that are personal to you.

This book is also for people who want their brilliant intelligence acknowledged, but can't afford to do a degree, or don't want to do one because of a bad experience with education, and the system that often tries to crush us, or just because the they don't like formal education or don't have the time.

It is also for people who no longer want to be a cog or a drone in the machine of industry or education. It teaches you how to get inspired, and to live the gift attaining life you so desire to live. Ok this book does make reference to Art, Illustration, Singing and Dance, and how I have utilised my talents in this area, but you can apply my teaching to any area that I have not mentioned. You can adapt this research to any field. It just requires a little creativity on your part.

BY READING THIS BOOK YOU WILL REDISCOVER HOW TO SING IN YOUR OWN VOICE, AND NOT THE VOICE OF THE SYSTEM.

It's about how you can make your own discoveries, that will bring you to the most beautiful wildest place in your career, a place that you could of never imagined. It's a book about how you can be original, and how you will never fully run out of ideas on how to make a success of your talents. The hard work is up to you though. I'm just giving you the recipe. It's up to you to do something creative with this research and to start to develop your own wings that will take your talent to areas you have always dreamed of, which is of course to recognise and achieve your gift, and to do something with the gift that will bless people, and enhance the experience of your own life in the process. Enjoy.

ENJOY YOUR GIFT

Chapter 1

THE FIRST LEG OF MY JOURNEY

This is not a book on how to draw, though the contents of which may inspire such action. It is not a book to compete with all the other archetypal art books displayed on coffee tables around the world.

This is a book that I intend to be remarkable.

But remarkable in whose eyes, mine, yours, my fans, no remarkable for its ability to inspire you to take up something for yourself, to be creative and help you get fired up, to help you find your creative path as a creative individual?

AND ONE WAY TO DO THAT IS TO TELL YOU THE STORY OF HOW I CAME TO CREATE THESE ILLUSTRATIONS....

Also in addition to my writing about the journey I took to create these illustrations, I will give examples of my progress in attaining my singing gift. I began singing seriously at the same time I decided to create a professional body of work for my Facebook fan page called Fashion Illustration Magazine. www.facebook.com/fashionillustrationmagazine . As I did both together I realised that there are strong parallels that exist between these two separate skills. Blending singing and illustration for me was the perfect choice, as I could do my scales and song practice at same time as drawing. Although sometimes one does take more importance, the body of work I developed for Fashion Illustration Magazine I did do whilst practicing singing. Prior to this body of work I just focused on my drawing. The idea is, when you have one skill under your belt, you can at times focus on two skills. But there is a point to just focus on one thing at a time to, you just have to be selective, decide for yourself when to choose. One may take more importance than the other; I am just saying work on both at the same time so you have a choice later on.

In addition to the research on illustration and singing, I learned that Pilates improves many aspects of your dance training too. Strength, stamina, and body alignment are vital for all sporting activity. Also having a physically fit well aligned body is really useful thing to have whilst you are trying to decide which sporting activity to specialise in. This study is about yourself getting a good grounding in many skills so you can specialise at a later date when you have made your decisions about what your gift is. If you already know what your gift is there still could be some good nuggets of information to help you take it to another level. Also if you have a gift already, there is no harm in trying to discover if you have another one that can blend beautifully with it.

So this work discusses how to improve your illustration, drawing, creative ideas, singing, musicianship, and physical strength, stamina. You take control of this yourself by following you own creative prompts.

    Although you can apply what I am teaching at anytime, and at whatever stage you are at, this research is geared for people who are stuck, or feel like giving up, and need advice in how to follow through on an idea with more attitude. Even if you take my advice for fun, you never know where it could lead you, to a new career, or even to a more fulfilled life, partaking in something creative just for the joy of it. This research is about you making an informed choice about how not to waste your time, when you desire to develop a talent. And it is also about how to get people who have talents in many areas to make a more informed choice about what to specialise in.

Chapter 2

DECIDING WHAT TO DO IN LIFE

Drawing for me has been a journey, a path, my own path. For years I studied at pre-degree level, occasionally doing private intensive courses in all things creative. I had thought about doing a degree but I couldn't truly decide what to do at degree level.

My theory was that I wasn't just one thing. I had skills in so many different areas and I enjoyed them all. Deciding what to do made me feel like a bird in a cage.

Also I felt like I needed a trade, something I could specialise in. Yet throughout my years of studying I hadn't learnt any technical independence away from the educational system. I had been spoon fed by the educational system and the only time I drew confidently was in relation to a course or a class. I couldn't just pick up a pencil and suddenly create a beautiful drawing for myself.

And what I personally mean by beautiful drawing or a piece of art was that it needed to be both beautiful and technically accurate in the creative sense of the word. Although later after getting my work technically accurate it freed me up to create more expressive work too that I was happy with. So I decided to study on my own, away from the system of education which I felt was holding me back as a creative individual. So I went to the library and studied the Great Artists and took notes. I read about the Pre-Raphaelites, the Renaissance (again) and various art movements, like the Bauhaus, Surrealism and biographies of the Great Artists.

YOU SEE I WANTED TO GET INSIDE THE MINDS OF THE GREATS AND SEE WHAT MADE THEM TICK....

The Greats doesn't have to be artists, it can be actors, choreographers, sportsmen and women, chefs, dancers, I am just using the Great Artist as an example.

I was fed up with teachers and the limitations I felt they had of me, and the time it was taking me to be brilliant at what I do. And what I mean by limitations is, more the limitations the teachers have in taking me where I wanted to go. And I kind of felt a degree wouldn't do this for me. So with this personally chosen knowledge which I was now gaining for free, I felt like I was beginning to grow wings.

APPLYING RELEVANT KNOWLEDGE...

And the thing is with knowledge is that you have to know how to apply it. Knowledge in itself isn't enough. You have to act on it with purpose. So after reading about forty art books, I started to draw. (more later on why I chose to do this)

Keeping in mind all the things I had learnt from the biographies of the Masters, I began to apply my knowledge. I did a lot of gesture drawing and I also copied in my own style and echoed the drawing language, of the Masters of art like Leonardo, Michelangelo, Renoir, Degas, Matisse, and Toulouse Lautrec.

You see during the Renaissance, the apprentices to the Great Masters always began by copying from masterpieces before they could be let into the studio.

And with this knowledge and with my persistence I started to feel like I was developing my own quality of line. When I felt my quality of line was getting there, I started to do close study.

And the close I study I did was from fashion photography, from magazines like Vogue, Marie Claire, Harper's Bazaar and Elle, as well as alternative magazine like ID magazine and Dazed. Although at this point I knew my close study was very good I knew at this point it wasn't outstanding. And later I began to draw accurately the drawings of famous artists too with more intention. I have always drawn from famous artist but in a casual way, this time round I was doing this more seriously but also fitting it in with writing this book and singing.

And also as I wanted to push my drawing into more conceptual ideas, I had to make time for thinking how my work would fit into the grand scheme of things, the complete idea.

I knew I still had to persue the line till it was perfect.

Chapter 3

TEACH YOURSELF INTUITIVELY FROM WITHIN

You see education is expensive, travel, fees, lunches. Yes you do get to spend time with other like minded people. But if you follow this advice you may find that this could a better alternative to doing a degree. Providing you already have the basic skills, you can begin to develop your gift. I did have the basic skills as I studied life drawing and did foundation courses. It doesn't have to be in drawing, it can be in sport, dance, choreography, painting, writing, set design, or any other type of design. Anything you aspire yourself to be, you can become. And this was the first step I took to begin to break myself free of the system, to study in this way independently.

And through this I discovered that I wasn't just a good drawer, that I had a gift. And I kept persuing this gift until I had reached a certain beauty I admired.

I was beginning to fight back at the system that had held me back, and made me fit into its mould. And yes I do believe that doing a degree would of held me back, perhaps even by three years.

I wouldn't be where I am today with this gift if I hadn't of followed my own path, I would of been a product of the system. Also, try not to take out any loans to pay for education, or buy materials, if necessary apply for grants and funding or do some kind of additional work to buy things you need. The whole point of this book is to make you think on the spot, to use what is available to you.

Use this time to teach yourself intuitively from within.

PUT YOURSELF ON A CREATIVE BUDGET....

If you are well off try putting yourself on a creative budget. Seriously, it's often the ones who start out broke who have the most success and inventive ideas. Materials will come. Money will come too. I was lucky with my talent, because with pencil drawing, the outlay was very miniscule. But I did set aside lots of art materials just in case I needed to add something or change my medium.

SELECTING THAT WHICH INSPIRES YOU....

You see this was my idea (an idea that becomes something that is) to draw, and draw, and draw, till I created lines that fitted together like a beautiful melody.

And it was in that melody of line that friends noticed that I had developed my gift.

You see this was something I could do for myself. I didn't just draw any fashion shoot, I drew ones that inspired me, and for this I had to go through hundreds and select favourites (I had so many that I had to keep a file of all of them, so I could draw them at a later date).

And it was in this drawing that I discovered something about the power of visualisation and previous study.

Before I put pencil to paper I had a picture in my mind of how it would turn out (often better). I had combined previous intellectual, practical and visual knowledge of historical and contemporary artistic styles and visualised it upon the modern fashion shoot how it was going to turn out. And it was with this visualisation that drove and inspired me to complete the drawings. Some drawings took hours, some took less long, but the prior vision of the outcome was what gave me the perseverance to complete it.

MY VISION WAS STRENGTH WITH SIMPLICITY, PURITY OF LINE, AND PASSION WITH EMOTION....

I drew from the fashion photograph how I visualised it. I was free. No one was telling me what to do, or how to do it. I was discovering something for myself. And in this discovery I found confidence as a woman, as an artist, and as a pioneer of something. I had an idea, to study the Great Artists, with the aspiration of creating something great myself. And this is only the beginning of my journey.

You see you have to understand, that sometimes the simplest pencil drawing can be the most beautiful, because of the study and the joyfulness of creating behind it. And my work was beginning to have the emotion, passion, simplicity and strength that I was looking for. Though later I developed more visions for my drawing style and I didn't just limit myself to one idea.

ENJOY YOUR GIFT

Chapter 4

YOUR INSPIRATION STARTS WITH THE VISUAL

FINDING YOUR INSPIRATION often starts with the visual. You see something like a piece of art, or an Olympic runner and you aspire to it. You start to copy. For a while this can bring a sense of enthusiasm and joy, but when the going gets tougher you need to formulate a plan and stick to it in order to achieve your goal. Some people can seem lucky, they go from inspiration, to action, to ultimate success, but if you look deeper there are struggles, doubts and failures to overcome, but ultimately the successful ones look to infinite intelligence or God to guide them.

They also have faith, and a vision guided by such, and they also have a strong determination to get to where they want to be. If you ever feel you are on the wrong path get onto the right path. You see by being on the right path, you will endeavour to see the realisation of your gift. Use your intuition to help guide you onto the right path for you.

THE REALIASTION OF YOUR GIFT WILL GIVE YOU WINGS, AND, DERTERMINED PEOPLE WANT TO FLY...

Determined people want to fly, and learning to fly can be hard work. Once you have achieved your goal, and that is to attain your gift (because everyone has a gift) you can turn your gift into a business or a job. And then you really will be flying.

WHEN YOU FEEL INSPIRED YOU ALSO FEEL PROMPTED....

You see when you feel inspired, you also feel prompted, to take up a class, take up a pencil, or paint, or take up running, singing, dance or fitness. It is important to follow this prompt; it is the creativity in you inspiring you to take action.

And if you ever feel yourself loosing the desire to take action, you have to find a way to fight yourself through this.

You see, if you take action in response to a prompt, you start to develop a vision. This vision can either be a set goal, or it could develop and change. Even if this vision does develop and change you are still going with the flow of creativity. Allow it to change, but still keep in mind your desire to develop your gift.

Also it is not unheard of to have a vision first and for someone to stick to it, this too can be combined with a prompt.

THE USE OF MIND MAPS...

Take a review of every creative, sporting, performance skill using mind mapping

I went from life drawing for years to then studying level 3 anatomy.

My independent study of anatomy did improve my art, though I did not make this connection at the time. Ideally find a class where you do life drawing that is combined with classical anatomy. If you can't find a class like this, combine it yourself.

And the thing is with the self development of your gift, you can always take a mind map of your skills like this. You can write '**SKILLS**' in the centre of the page and start to make links. You can also write '**THINGS I ENJOY DOING**' and '**THINGS I AM BEST AT**', and if you make links with all these areas, this will be a very beneficial exercise. It could also be wise to mind map '**ALL BUSINESS ADVISE I HAVE BEEN GIVEN**'. You can also make up your own relevant titles as this will further encourage independent thinking. You could also have a mind map entitled '**WHAT I THINK**'. This type of mind mapping can bring you focus and sense of purpose, and be the first step in helping you develop your vision.

This type of mind mapping can create prompts for you to act on, on the pathway to developing your gift....

You can do this in the area of sport, dance, art, writing, designing, music, as well as many other areas, even in cooking.

ENJOY YOUR GIFT

Chapter 5

YOUR OWN HEART IS WHERE YOUR UNIQUENESS LIES

REMEMBER YOUR OWN CREATIVE PATH COMES FROM YOUR HEART; YOUR HEART IS WHERE YOUR OWN UNIQUENESS LIES....

You see with my writing I am not teaching you how to draw. There are thousands of books out there that can do that for you.

I am not interested in someone becoming a carbon copy of my drawing style; I am interested in someone developing their gift.

You see if you did a degree or a modular course you are still doing the work to please the course leaders, the course devisors, or the system.

Modules don't come from the heart. Your own creative path comes from the heart. The game is to discover where your creative path lies.

If doing a degree gives you the experience and the freedom to develop your gift from the heart, and not become a product of the college, then do this. But also, for your self esteem and that of your peers, it is a good idea to try and get good grades, if you do decide to do a course.

Yet at the same time, if exploring means getting lower grades, exploring is preferential, as you never know where the exploration can take you. Also failing a course can give you the impetus to find your own path. Again follow your instinct and you intuition on this matter. I failed my A level art, but I never let that stop me, and I believe it was because I was exploring the drawing and not doing what was required of me.

And it's is far cheaper nowadays to reflect on my method of doing things. If you get stuck, go to a professional teacher and get unstuck, then continue on your path. If you work in this way, with perseverance and self discipline you will attain your gift. Also by gaining many relating skills and applying them inventively and intuitively, you could if you wanted to, start on year two of a degree. You could even surpass a degree and go straight on to a Masters.

Alexander McQueen studied tailoring a Saville Row and did tailoring as a job there, this experience allowed him to go straight onto a masters without having to do a degree (Alexander Mc queen is the top fashion house, who's house designed the wedding dress for the Royal Wedding of the Duke and Duchess of Cambridge). And in this day and age of expensive tuition and educational brainwashing, my advice is worth far more than the many thousands you will save. And you will have the advantage of not having a huge debt over your head, freeing you to start your business from a fresh perspective.

KEEP REREADING TREASURED BOOKS THAT CREATIVELY GUIDE YOU

If necessary keep rereading my book till you understand my message, and if you get a prompt, take action, keep following through. Prompts to do things can be quite repetitive, following your prompts, is like having your own teacher inside your soul guiding you, sometimes on a daily moment by moment basis. Keep rereading my book to guide you, inspire you to help you reach your ultimate goal which is to attain your gift. And once you have your gift, keep reading this, and other inspiring words and books, to remind you to keep moving forward. Or you could just follow you intuition without a book like this, many people have, I am just writing this for people who need this and disagreeing with the contents can prompt you onto further achievements far beyond my talents. That is what a book like this should be about, you surpassing my ideas and bringing something to the next generation.

Remember a degree teaches you how to pass modules; your gift will give you wings.

Some people, study do their hobby or pastime for years before they see the beauty of their gift emerge.

This all depends on your story or your journey, don't give up, stick with it.

Some people have a gift, but they haven't discovered the market for it, don't give up, stick with it, keep at it. Keep in mind the people or the thing you aspire to, as this will motivate you beyond measure.

ENJOY YOUR GIFT

Chapter 6

FAILURE WHAT'S THAT?

THERE IS NO SUCH THING AS FAILURE IN THE CREATIVE WORLD, AS EVERYTHING IS RELEVANT.

While you are trying to discover your gift, you will go through all sorts of stages.

And you will know when you have discovered your gift, something inside tells you.

EXPLORATORY STAGE VERSES THE FOCUSED STAGE: ONE

You will always need to be aware of the stages of attaining your gift. First there is the exploratory/discovery stage, where you try lot of different things. Some people do go straight into doing what their gift is, because some people just know.

The second stage to attaining your gift is the focused stage. These two stages of exploring, and then focusing, both require you to give your whole heart time and energy. It is in the giving of your whole heart, time and energy that you will begin to see results.

Never be lazy. It may take years of hard work to attain your gift, if it does, don't be discouraged, because in those years you are building a strong foundation. And also if you take years to discover your gift, the skills and the experience that you have received over this time will give you a strong foundation. And too remember although I have written this book I still haven't completely arrived, I am still on the journey too. I am just sharing my experience to help you find your own journey. My journey isn't your journey, though my journey can inspire your journey

Also many gifts can be blended beautifully if you know how and this book will show you how. Blending a few gifts will take longer than just focusing on just one, at a time. Another thing is when you have got your gift, don't stop keep working hard to reach higher levels of your talent. This payoff will be remarkable. Everything you do is relevant and there is no such thing as failure when you are on a creative path.

You can learn from every experience and blend every skill that you have learnt along the way.

Nothing is wasted. I took a detour and spent time making some handmade cards out of ribbon and embroidery thread and this has inspired a new way to illustrate.

EXPLORATION STAGE VERSES THE FOCUSED STAGE: TWO

And yes it is ok to be a jack of all trades and a master of nothing. This can be called the exploration stage, the finding out stage, the stage you are at, before you commit to a skill.

But it is better to take a review of all your trades and to be a master of one thing, perhaps two or if your super talented three or four. This is a book about you taking a view of all your skills to help you make a commitment to one or two or three skills, and to follow through. Knowing where you are at with your skill really does help.

Often we will go from the focused stage, back to the exploration stage, then back to the focused stage, many times before we see that little sparkle from our work that tells us we've arrived. And if you are really true to your art, you will always be exploring, and always focusing, and expressing. And you can continue to do this well into your professional career.

And that's the beauty of this journey, it never ends, we are always discovering. And since writing this I have developed so much as an artist and I feel like I know myself and where my life is going. And that is what I wish for you.

ENJOY YOUR GIFT

Chapter 7

CREATING A GIFT THAT PEOPLE SEEK OUT

If you are developing your gift, you need to almost see it as a product or interest that people will seek out. You need in the early stages of attaining your gift, to think about how to bring it to market. Look at others in a similar area to you, and decide how you are going to blend your gift with the commercial world. And remember as I have said before the commercial world is changing.

ART FOR ARTS SAKE OR ART FOR A LIVING

And I know how much some artists shy away from making big money, because some believe that by doing this that they are not being true to their art if they do it for gain. This is called art for art sake. Remember it is still a worthy path to be on. And although I have written about making money I recently discovered that I am one of those artists who is doing art for art's sake. Nevertheless you could be an artist who is meant to make money right now and I hope this book can help you.

Well, I'm hoping my ideas will help to free you from this belief, if you feel stuck in this belief,   because if you are following your prompts, the enjoyment and the gain will blend so beautifully, that you will never feel like you lost your soul in the process. Blending the design of the gift in the early stages of its attainment, with the current market we are now in, is a skill worth learning even if you are an art for art's sake artist. Every gift area is different, so you will have to make that discovery for yourself.

If your slant on your gift is unique, and original, people will seek you out. But you will have to let the ones that like original ideas (early adopters), and who like to share original products, creativity and ideas know about it first.

SHOW YOU'RE WORK TO THE WORLD WHEN IT IS READY, NOT BEFORE.

ONLY USE SOCIAL MEDIA SITES FOR RESEARCH, NEVER SHARE YOUR WORK HERE UNTIL YOU ARE AT A PROFESSIONAL STANDARD, OR AN ALMOST PROFFESSIONAL STANDARD.

 I say this for the sake of your career, as it is very hard to go from a good artist to an outstanding artist in the public eye. Don't show any of your developmental work on these sites. You can show work to mentors and close friends, but it is better to show in person, not via social networking. You have to realise that developmental work is personal.

Also when showing work on social media sites try not to show it at an angle, photograph it face on and just the paper no edges and not materials in view. It will look more professional and you will get more likes and traffic to your page. Watermarks can spoil a work, as with big signatures too. Keeping a signature discrete shows the work off to its best advantage as with discrete watermarks too. Small initials are better. Save work when scanned in both PDF and JPEG format. Amazon prefer a PDF of your images when creating books. Knowing this saves time. When you put work on online media sites for viewing, lower the DPI, as this protects your image a bit. Ask your local printers for advice on this in case this advice changes. This is what I do, and what is right for your art work and the latest technology could be different. Do not put PDF's on social media sites unless you want people to have access to a high resolution image. If you do, use a watermark.

Ok you need to share for feedback, but you also need to keep a sense of mystery to your work. Having early work alongside more professional work can be confusing to the viewer. Some pages on facebook have this and my advice is to delete them. You need to have a body of work that is of the same high standard and of a shared consistency.

Try not to throw away work that is a study or a good example of a finished piece, as you do need to remind yourself of how far you have come too.

Practice makes your work fascinating and outstandingly beautiful.

REMEMBER THE MORE YOU PRACTICE THE MORE FACINATING YOUR STUDIES WILL BECOME.

Even my studies are not the same standard of that of the Masters, pick up any art book and you will see that these studies are breathtaking. Their studies are outstanding, mine are exploratory though I am still learning their language like learning a singing style I am learning a drawing style by copying. My studies are not shown on facebook as they are personal to me. My studies will get more brilliant, but this will take time. Also always check your work before uploading it, to see it is in proportion.

Look at professional dancers and the dance studies that they make with top choreographers, they are brilliant, and it is still a study. If you want to become brilliant at something, to make the study just as outstanding, and just as beautiful, as the finished piece, practice, practice, practice, and practice some more too. Don't get content with compliments. Once someone says you are good at something, and it isn't outstanding yet, it could put pay to ambition, and the attainment of your true gift. Once someone says you are good at something you could stop trying to be better. Just say thank you for the compliment and keep in mind your ambition.

PRACTICE IS A JOYFUL THING TO DO, AND YOU WILL SEE RESULTS NO MATTER WHAT.

It does take time, and depending on where you are at, and where you want to get to, is the time that it will take. You have to decide how you are going to practice, and how you are going to maximise the results you desire to achieve. This is what my book is about, maximising the results in illustration/drawing, dance practice, and singing/music practice.

The skills that I am going to impart to you can be adapted to other fields, but I can only share the fields that I have proven results and experience in. As I said before, adapting my advice to your area, takes a little creativity on your part and I wish you to achieve the best results in the safest way possible.

ENJOY YOUR GIFT

Chapter 8

KEEP AN EYE ON YOUR GOAL

KEEP AN EYE ON YOUR GOAL AT ALL TIMES, AND DON'T BE CONTENT WITH COMPLIMENTS IN THE EARLY STAGES OF ATTAINING YOUR GIFT, SELECT ADVICE VERY CAREFULLY.

We all have a gift, keep in mind that you want to develop it and not just get random compliments for a gift that isn't even born yet. This advice is for people who are serious about going professional with their gift. Some people may decide to use their gift as a satisfying hobby. By all means show your work to close friends, your advisors, and mentors, because success can be in the council of many.

Never rely on one piece of advice, it could be wrong.

I was told by a mentor to give up my drawing and go into fashion design because it could make me more money, but it isn't about the money. It's about what I love to do. And I do feel personally I didn't want to pollute the environment with the residues of pollutants from a fashion factory. That is why I took the art for art's sake route. And it hasn't been an easy choice but I felt in my soul having a business that pollutes the environment would go against my love for animals and the world. But by all means develop the skills of a fashion designer as you could find a solution to this problem if you follow your prompts.

The thing is I could draw all day but I couldn't sew all day, I enjoy designing fashion, but I don't really like intricate sewing for commercial purposes. I didn't want to spend hours on something that could be eaten by moths, only to be in its glory in the form of a much loved photograph. That was just my opinion, but your gift could be to create beautiful fashion designs, it is just I'm not a fan of sewing. Though later I may create a fashion show just not at the moment. And too some fashion designs are worshiped like great pieces of art.

I wanted to create something that would give lasting inspiration to generations, like the Masters of Art.

I know this is a huge ambition, but I could be just a few years away from this, if I work really hard, this is only the beginning. You see that comment about giving up drawing did discourage me, and I did take another path. I did try designing again. But I missed doing my art and I also decided my art had potential, so I once again to pursued the line till it was perfect. Yes I may of wasted time going back into designing, but this change of direction gave me the impetus to try beyond measure to get good at my illustrating. Don't listen to people it could set you back, and if you know what you want to do already don't listen to me either.

And I did bring myself up to this level without a teacher guiding me, using my own hard work, past and present knowledge, skill and determination. I was trained in drawing but my skills as an illustrator and having something substantial to post on social media or show in a gallery wasn't quite to my standard.

You see I did have lots of advice given to me, and this did confuse me at times, I decided to shuffle it around till it suited me. I did this with note taking, mind mapping and action, and so far it has paid off. You see advisors are not always right, doing the opposite of what they say, can sometimes be the best decision. This includes doing the opposite to what I say or not listening at all. I so cringe at books that claim to know the way, I am just sharing my way and I hope it helps you to find your own way that is all.

Always shuffle advice around in order to find what suits you.

MAKING YOUR GIFT PAY AND MAINTAINING REGULAR EMPLOYMENT....

Anyway if you already have your gift you may be wondering how to make it pay. If you have gained qualifications on how to teach (adult education classes have a City & Guilds teaching certificate PTLES that you can do in one or two terms), this can be a useful way to fund yourself till you find a niche market for your gift. There are plenty of part time jobs that pay well, if you look and use your imagination. And sometimes their flexibility will give you the free time to work on your gift attaining skills. Well, if you want to make it pay, you will find a way, you just have to keep trying and pushing. There is no one way to make your gift pay, if you seek higher wisdom you will be shown the way. If you are working or doing alternative study, you may find you will have to put in a lot of hours outside this to make your gift develop. If the gift you wish to attain compliments from the current job you are already doing, this extra- curricular activity as shown in this book, could go down well on your CV and put you in line for promotion. It could also go down well to put you in line for a job with a company that is more highly paid or has better prospects.

Highly paid doesn't always mean better if you are not following your dream.

Always aim for the job with better creative prospects, as the money will come, trust me.

And if the job does have better prospects, try to choose a job that is in line with your dream and your gift. If the gift you want to attain compliments your current study you are doing, don't rush and give up your studies. Put in the extra hours if you can, as the information in this book could help you get the best out of your studies, if there isn't a teacher there to answer the questions you need answering.

But bear in mind, fully taking the advice in this book and getting the results you desire should be treated like a full time job. And doing the opposite or totally ignoring what I say should be treated like a full time job. (I hope you enjoy my humour). I treated it as a full time job taking this advice, my own advice, and you can see what I have achieved. Treating the advice in this book like a full time job, and taking on part time work during your free time is the best advice I can give you, if you are really dedicated. There is always a way, it is up to you to find it.

ENJOY YOUR GIFT

Chapter 9

ALWAYS BE PROACTIVE

Remember though, for some, it is necessary to do course in all things creative, as this could be part of the journey in attaining your gift. Just choose your courses wisely so that you don't waste your time. By all means get involved in education, this isn't a book that is about being anti-education, it is about attaining your gift. Choose teachers wisely, so that you will have the freedom to do so much more with your life. Your gift can bless and inspire others, sharing your experience of attaining your gift can also bless and inspire you. You see the reason I never did a degree was because I felt that doing a degree would still give me the same results as my pre-degree study., and that was cupboards full of art work that doesn't have a niche place in this world. Fashion Illustration Magazine became my niche world. www.facebook.com/fashionillustrationmagazine .

I was not a hoarder, I was a proactive person, who didn't know how to make things work for myself outside the system, until I got away from the system and started to do some thinking for myself about my situation as an artist. Creative people are not designed for factory like employment. Although some famous artists do have studios that produce work in a factory like environment like Jeff Koons.

And this has paid off for me no end, and I am grateful that I took this step of faith and arrived at where I am today.

My experience is creativity, and drawing, yours may be something else, but it doesn't mean that you can't get something from my experience, and apply it to your journey.

Sometimes the thought of rigorous dance training is good energy that can be applied to rigorous drawing days.

Drawing can have the same intensity that a dancer goes through during training, or prep for an audition. It's the same energy, just a different skill applied in a different way. And yes it can be good to leap around a studio painting, as long as it is focused, as this could be good physical preparation for set painting for theatres or huge murals too.

ENJOY YOUR GIFT

Chapter 10

BE EXTRAORDINARY

NEVER RUN WITH THE CROWD, YOUR LIFE WILL BE MORE EXTRAORDINARY FOR NOT DOING SO. You see the message of this book is too teach you not to run with the crowd, because if you do that you will always stay with the crowd. But staying with the crowd if they are a good crowd, could be the best most brilliant thing for you, you will know in your heart what is right for you, and this book is about helping you find the freedom to know what that is.

Marcel Duchamp created work that was anti the art establishment, but in doing so he has found a way to fit nicely into it, and he became the father of conceptual art.

You may seem to be unique and individual within the system, but it's those who step away from the system who really do stand out. Again as I say this is open to opinion, sometimes the system works for people.

BEING FOCUSED AND EXPRESSED....

You see the journey to attain your gift is a creative one, and your creativity needs to be both focused and expressed. Both at the same time and separately, when it is expressed you are exploring, though there is still an element of exploration in focused activity. When it is both focused and expressed you are making plans to develop your vision and improve your chances of attaining your gift.

It's the clever ones that reign in creativity and make it work for them.

And once you have attained your gift, you can move onto more advanced creativity by formulating a plan that is a higher level than your previous plan. My next book will be about this. And again, you do this with further reading, mind mapping, and note taking, and other relevant activity.

The path of creativity is a never ending one, enjoy the journey.

ENJOY YOUR GIFT

Chapter 11

THE POWER OF VISUALISATION

UTILISE THE POWER OF KNOWLEGE AND VISUALISATION. The two of the most powerful forces combined is the use of favourable knowledge and visualisation. They become a force to be reckoned with when combined with action, which is another powerful force. Think favourable knowledge, visualisation then action, then the powerhouse for your dreams is yours. As Louis Pasteur said 'Chance favours the prepared mind'. Well, my version of that is...

'Favourable knowledge empowers visualisation, for creative gift action'.

You increase your chances in everything if you have the right knowledge, and if it's in the creative fields you can develop this knowledge without formal teaching if you have the basics, though some fields of creativity do require specialist teaching.

But it's your desire to read relevant books that will give substance to your creativity and your gift.

Sometimes a relevant course can be used as spring board for you to develop your gift, but it is the self directed learning that usually brings out the uniqueness of your talent.

APPRECIATE ALL THE STEPS YOU TAKE....

Every step is a beautiful journey, love every step, love it like it is your own child developing, growing, blossoming, or if you prefer, a shrub, or a tree you take pride in.

It may take many years to attain your dream, like it can take years to grow up, or grow shrubs or a tree from seed, tend to your every step like you are nurturing something delicate. Take pleasure in what you gain, and gaze at the endeavour of your results with delight.

By delighting in each step you take, creates a wonderful energy, as you watch your gift mature into its full fruition, as you put in the hard work and hours required.

LISTEN TO YOUR FEELINGS....

Your feelings are God's gift, they are the silent speakers of your soul that guide you, comfort you, and show you how to intelligently make productive decisions.

Take time out to try to feel where your feelings are coming from. Feelings don't always come from the heart. That can be a cliché. They can come from your feet to dance, your hands to draw or create, or your fingers to tap out a particular rhythm, or your voice to sing a song or say something.

But it is often the heart that does feel like it is the motor of your desires.

So if your desire is to swim, run, draw, paint, sing, dance, act, create music, or a theatre production, do this feel this, and keep doing what you feel creatively, and ideas will come true goals will be set, and you will develop the purpose for being on this planet.

IMAGINE YOURSELF ATTAINING YOUR GIFT.

Spend 5 minutes every day or more imagining yourself attaining yourself at your final milestone, either a Gold Medal at the Olympics, critical acclaim for a book, a gallery exhibition, or a dance or a film you are part of, or even a dance company you own.

The imagination is powerful. It sends nerve impulses from your brain to your body that gives you that impulse and desire to take action. It can pull universal strings that work in your favour.

Sometimes all you have is your imagination, and this can be even more powerful than all the people who tell you to give up on your dream, remember this as it will encourage you.

It is a beautiful gift that gives you the ability to succeed, even at that critical moment, like becoming first in a race. The imagination can fire adrenaline to make you run faster or work harder. It can also help you to produce endorphins which make the endeavour pleasurable (not exactly proven, but I do believe this). The imagination can help get rid of frustration of rushing to achieve, and it can help you to enjoy every step, and piece of progress that you make. But focus on your goal to become a particular standard, it could be to become very good, excellent, or the best in the world..... You decide..... But if you reach a talent plateau and feel you can't go beyond this, either enjoy where you are, or try finding a way to go beyond this plateau.

THE IMAGINATION IS THE POWER TO MAKE IT HAPPEN....

THE PERSON WITH THE DREAM THAT THEY LENT TO THEIR IMAGINATION IS THE ONE WITH THE POWER TO MAKE IT HAPPEN.

Dreams and the imagination go hand in hand, but it is the imagination that inspires action.

The dream is the decision you make before you lend it to your imagination.

The idea is often the source of inspiration, you dream about your idea, but once the dream has been lent to your imagination, the imagination takes over and that's where the magic begins.

That's why they say dreamers are dead, because the dreamer won't let go, and give the imagination a chance to muster up its magic, and with direct positive action, help you understand what you are made of. The imagination is a tough cookie, and the dreamer can be a bit fluffy, and if you are bored of being fluffy, bored of people laughing at you, give your dream to your imagination, because trust me, combined with intelligent action, it will never let you down. You see people will laugh at you, even if you do take that step, and give your dream to your imagination. But if you are persistent, you could be one of those people who have a sweet little smile on your face, because you are going somewhere, and they are not. Dreamers are the ones who often say 'I wish' but the ones who lend their dream to their imagination are the ones who say 'I did'. And it feels so much better saying 'I did' than saying ' I wish' isn't it.

ENJOY YOUR GIFT

Chapter 12

CHOOSE BEING CREATIVE OVER BEING RIGID

ALWAYS CHOOSE BEING CREATIVE....

Being creative is beautiful, it flows like a stream, and it melts like snow, being rigid stinks. If you let go, and let happen, beauty appears, in a desire to dance, or sing, or run, or anything that is worthy of inspiration. There is something beautiful in the ever flowing joy of creation, your own personal creation.

Appreciating creation, or the universe, whatever your belief, will put you in touch with the creative forces that make things happen.

These creative forces can be your own personal evolution or your connection to the Creator himself. Whatever is personal to you, will work, after all some believe God created evolution, some believe we evolved from nothingness, but as a creative person, you are constantly evolving into your true potential as a creative human being.

It is much more fun to feel the creative energy flow through your body, that's where ideas happen, dreams are dreamt, and once given to the imagination, where the magic begins.

The small steps will multiply...

IT'S THE SMALL STEPS THAT YOU TAKE, THAT WILL MULTIPLY INTO YOUR GIFT....

Congratulate yourself for every milestone passed on the road to attaining your gift.

Smile at your progress.

It is a wonderful feeling to know you are achieving something.

It is even more wonderful when you know that the steps you have taken are your own personal steps. And not that of a course you have been brainwashed or told to do. Unless it's something like private one to one tuition, as this type of training can be different from formal education. Small steps lead to bigger things. Big things lead to bigger dreams, and the bigger your imagination, the harder you will need to work to achieve what you want to achieve.

Choosing the more difficult path will bring you the best reward that you could have ever imagined. This is a difficult path, but a rewarding one too. Even though it was difficult, I still saw it as simple, because in some ways it is both, difficult and simple.

ENJOY YOUR GIFT

Chapter 13

MOVE WITH THE TIMES AND BE A PIONEER

GET OUT OF YOUR COMFORT ZONE AND BECOME AWARE THAT TIMES HAVE CHANGED. This will help you get onto the path for attaining your gift. Keep up with what is current, that way you won't waste your time, down the road that has less prospects. Being aware of the times, moving with the times, and even being a pioneer of the times, will bring you a joy and a satisfaction that you will never be able to explain.

CREATE SOMETHING THAT IS RELEVANT....

And a bonus of that is, when you are creating something that is relevant, you will experience the joy of people being actually able to understand you, and that is something money cannot buy.

ANYTHING IS POSSIBLE....

LAW OF GRAVITY, THE LAW OF ECONOMICS, AND 'THE CULTURE OF THE GIFT'....

Just as we have a law of gravity which we cannot fight not matter how powerful or clever we become, we also can't oppose the law of economics. It's just that the law of economics has evolved, and opposing this evolution will just bring heartache and pain.

We need to embrace this change and to embrace it now.

We have expected this economic system to be constant like gravity, and yes it is constant but it's taking on a new form due to the World Wide Web. This new form is partly to do with blogging. We have forgotten about the history of money and commerce, and how it has developed over the centuries. And we have believed that we will be trapped by the system for the rest of our lives. This is not the case, the world has changed. The law of gravity is constant, the cycle of the moon is constant, the position of the stars are constant, but the law of attraction is constant, but the law of economics is always evolving, if not slowly, it is still open to change. And the beautiful thing is, that all this anger and hatred some people have had against the system will disappear for us, once we embrace 'The Culture of the Gift' that is just emerging. If we continue to do things the old way, it will feel like the forces are against us.

What we should be asking ourselves is, 'What are we going to do about it?' and 'How are we going to join this new tribe of creative's and artists who are now changing the world?'

Economics has changed, and we are to ask ourselves 'what are we going to do about it?' till answers appear. And when we begin to embrace this new change, our own lives will change in the process. By exploring 'The Culture of the Gift' we will begin to do this, and by embracing this change, we will begin to change our lives forever. And the thing is if 'The Culture of the Gift' does happen more collectively than it is happening now, we will have support. And there will be tribes of creative people giving amazing unique unexpected talent, from all walks of life back into society.

And yes we do need cheep disposable nick- knacks, but with this new culture there will be a new interest in quality, beauty and durableness of products, it could create a less throwaway society, if we embrace quality and 'The Culture of the Gift'.

Has anyone ever thought about designing a washing machine that is so iconic in design, that it will be eternally mended and never be thrown away apart from parts that no longer work, because we find it too beautiful to part, with like a vintage car. Ok maybe that will never happen.

But we also believed once we could never fly. Anything is possible. You just have to think about it first...

SWOT ANALYSE YOUR GIFT AND IT'S DEVELOPMENT....

Swot analyse isn't just for your business plan, it can be used for the development of your gift. You need to know what is out there, who's better than you, who you aspire too, and how different, similar, or original you are to your competitors. A gift isn't something that is fluffy and sweet, it is a critical tool in this dog eat dog world that we live in. Having an original gift will put food on the table, if you market it right. You are more than a hobbyist, you will at this point, maybe, stopped seeing friends that are bringing you down, and turned your life upside down.

ENJOY YOUR GIFT

Chapter 14

MODERN CONTENTMENT VERSES OLD FASHIONED CONTENTMENT

BE AWARE OF THIS PROCESS AND THE RIGHT PEOPLE WILL COME INTO YOUR LIFE.

And you will be far more content then you could ever imagine.

'Hmmm content' I hear you say. Well I don't mean content 'Lazy' I mean 'Content work like hard baby'. Content nowadays means, that in this ever changing market you have to work hard to stay content, and content isn't a feeling that stays the same, there are different levels of contentment, and being bored with your moments of contentment, will drive you to achieve more, and experience a new level of contentment. Contentment no longer means I've achieved something. Contented people know that in order to keep that feeling they have to be ready with the next project (that's why they have a sweet little smile on their face).

Old fashioned contentment can lead to panic, when you realise that the world has left you behind...

THE ART OF AIMING HIGH, CONSIDER IT AN ART.... and never being satisfied will help you aim high.

BE TRUE TO YOUR SUBJECT AND DON'T BE AFRAID TO BE WRONG...

Be true to your subject. Go beyond the consensus of what is considered right.

Dare to be wrong. And know that the creative path is one that is going to beyond your experience. That is why it is exciting, to go beyond your own experience, as this is where new discoveries are found.

Aiming high doesn't always mean travelling the same path as others that have aimed high, that path could be a well worn path. It's about looking at the people who have succeeded and creating a new map, your own one. The game has changed. During the past ten years, creative people have been moving out of the industrial age, into a new horizon which has a far nicer platform for their skills. The factory has changed from the actual factory, to the offices of commerce, i.e. call centres and insurance offices. Machines now do the work of the people of the Industrial Age.

USE YOUR PASSION TO CREATE YOUR OWN CREATIVE STORY...

We are Post-Industrial, which means we have more opportunity now to build our own little niche markets. In some ways we are almost going back in time, where we are able to reinvent the proverbial cottage industries, but for the new internet age of personal niche markets. Instead of being confined to our villages, we can network our niche markets to the global villages, expanding our experience. In this new and expanding market, we are creating new communities, new opportunities to share our gift, and creating opportunities for ideas to a happen. And the secret to this is the passion. And it is with this passion that you create your story. And it's the story behind your gift that will create a platform for your gift, giving it more substance.

If you can find the time to communicate your story to others alongside your gift, you will be sailing. And in the form of a book you could make money

It's all about the story, the gift, and the niche; you have to find your way to blend this, to make it fascinating.

To some this comes naturally, to others through inspiration, or a lot of hard work.

Whatever it takes, it will be worth it in the end.

KEEP REREADING TREASURED BOOKS....

Treasured books will keep you focused.

This mini chapter speaks for itself, and there is a lot to be said for this, life can be very busy and very distracting. If you keep rereading books that have a message and guide you, it will help you stay on track. Rereading paragraphs and chapters till you understand it, is a fabulous way to develop your mind.

If it's a new concept, rereading a new chapter till you grasp and understand it exercises your intelligence, and then next time you will find these concepts and chapters in other books a breeze.

Keep persisting with your reading no matter what stage you are at, never be lazy, you will see results and this will amaze you. You haven't truly read something until you have understood it, remember this. By reading and reading you and understanding what you have read, develops your mind in preparation for your art.

Also the more you understand something, you can cross reference with your own ideas, this is how you develop your mind, you don't need to do a degree to do that.

Chapter 15

THE MAGICIANS HAT

SHOW OTHERS HOW TO PULL THE PROVERBIAL RABBIT OUT OF THE MAGICIANS HAT (but not straight away). I have shown you how to create your own magic, and when you have found your own formula, maybe a variation of my wisdom, you can create your own form of communication around it and make a career out of it.

And by communication I mean, that you have your gift, and you can start sharing it with others.

But you must remember to not show the public or even close friends before it is at the standard you want, as it could ruin the surprise. Ok I showed my pre-gift work to my friends, but my collection that I spent four months on, I kept away from social media friends and other friends until I displayed it on my Facebook fan page. And I feel kind of lucky that I kept my pre-gift work in a neat folder, as this is proof that this idea does work.

I call this work my pre-gift work as my past work didn't really have a niche that it fitted into. Your work may already have a niche and that great, so this book will give you other ideas that will help improve your niche.

KEEP YOURSELF ALERT FOR CREATIVE OPPORTUNITIES.

MORE ON THE IMPORTANCE OF READING AND BEING ON THE ALERT, FOR CREATING YOUR OWN OPPORTUNITIES.

Ford didn't invent the car he just created a method of manufacture that made having a car more accessible and cheaper.

With me, I didn't create education, I just found a way to educate myself that was free, and suited what was accessible to me.

Bear in mind I did years of education and this book is about me creating a niche with my skills.

A few years ago I told someone that I wanted to read Van Gogh's autobiography, then this someone said 'If you read it, it will change the way you draw'. Bells clanged and clashed in mind, as I started to think, if this is the case then why do a degree? (I was thinking about all the money I was going to save). But also they forgot to mention drawing directly from photographs of famous artists too improves your drawing, this is what I have gotten more into recently, although you should combine this with drawing from your favourite Masters too.

It took me a good few years to find the time to put this into practice. It could take you time to put this book into practice too, but my advice is to act now. Anyway, as I don't like to do things by half's I decided to read around forty art books over a period of three months. I was putting in around 150 to 200 hours of reading a month, around 30 to 50 hours a week; this included rereading paragraphs I didn't understand. I read huge book on Italian Sculpture and Architecture, on Dali and Impressionism. I read about Art Nouveau and Art Deco, the Bauhaus, everything. And I took notes pages of notes; I also went to art exhibitions and took notes aswel.

I really enjoyed this time. It was very rewarding, and I had fabulous conversations with people, and I found I was beginning to feel quite proud of myself.

And after this time I started to draw again. I drew from the books that I read from, and I also drew from fashion shoots, I did both gesture and close study, but I kept my close study free and expressive as I was still developing the quality of line. During this time I reflected on all the things I had been taught and I reflected on the drawing techniques I was using now.

One drawing technique I became fond of was this...

When I was on an art foundation, attending an untaught life drawing session, one of my visiting friends decided to teach the class. During this time the college I was at focused very much on using charcoal. My friend stepped in and said why don't I draw the figure with a 2H pencil and sharpen it every now and again. This college didn't mind us drawing with blunt pencils. After the class my friend said, 'There that's better isn't it'. And it was I still have this drawing. I later discovered the joy of blending different pencils like 2H with 2B so no advice is ever set in stone, take advice and develop it, take this advice and develop it, just keep moving forward in your discoveries.

It was a simple but effective solution, he was a graphic artist my friend.

Note someone from a more graphic background may need to loosen up with Chinese brush and charcoal techniques.

I have recently learnt the joys of blending 2H pencils with 2B pencils in a really effective way. Best thing to do as a drawer is to get familiar with many drawing techniques and use this to your advantage. You do this by copying from the Masters.

Note: If you are a graphic artist you may want to do the opposite and create a more expressive line with materials like charcoal.

LOOK OUT FOR THIS...

FORMULATE A CREATIVE PLAN OF ACTION...

Anyway, my point here is, often it's taking what a teacher says and taking it to the extreme that will get results, and sometimes even if you are at a prestigious college doesn't mean the way they teach you matches your skills and talent. So anyway, it's all about looking out for these 'One Sentence's' that will change things for you, you just have to be aware and awake for the opportunity. And it is never too late to respond to a great idea, and if you feel stuck, get yourself unstuck with action and mind mapping/note taking and formulate a plan.

I did, and so can you. And the more you share the more the universe gives you more ideas, till your basket is overflowing

More reasons to follow your own path.

If you follow a path that has been set out for you by others, when it all goes wrong you can blame them.

This is no fun.

It's much better to take charge of your own path, and if it goes wrong, learn from your failure and this will help you grow into a mature independent human being.

Failures are stepping stones, use this false path as a stepping stone to your true path. This could even mean stepping off this set of stepping stones, walking down the river, and finding a nice bank, and building your own set of stepping stones, and creating a path that no one has ever trod on before, that being creative. And your prompts will help you do this. And if you do follow someone else's path, even if it is the path of a well meaning friend or relative, you will become a cog or a drone, of their dream for you. It's their dream for you, not your dream for you.

You have to be following your dream, this is so vital, and if you have been around a lot of people telling you how to live your life, you have to be strong and tell them where to go.

Always ask yourself, 'Is it my dream I'm following, or someone else's?'

Also if someone is intimidating you to follow a dream, tell them where to go, and that you are thinking for yourself now. This does happen. They have no right to do this to you. You create your own beauty in your life by following your own dream. **Be strong and stick with it.**

ENJOY YOUR GIFT

Chapter 16

THE ART OF SKY GAZING

TRY SKY GAZING TO RECHARGE YOUR BATTERIES.

When you are reading interesting books, and doing interesting things, like all the things I have suggested in this book, you will meet a lot of new people and make a lot of new friends. You will have to be very selective, because they could either encourage you, or distract you, or worse, stop you from responding to your prompts to get things done.

And you have to decide what you need, a day out socialising, an inspiring day out by yourself, or 15 hours of hard work at home or in a studio or sports facility, with no distractions.

Leaving your phone at home and having a chill day out by yourself can help you no end, if you can delegate responsibilities to others. Even putting your phone chip in an old style phone so you have no distractions from Facebook or Twitter, yet you can be contacted via phone is a good idea too.

When you are on your phone all the time you can forget the joy of living in the moment.

I did this and I rediscovered the joy of watching cloud formations in the sky change like a really sleepy kaleidoscope of sky blue and cotton wool white.

And trust me doing this is an art, and it recharged my batteries no end.

I had a dream...

ALWAYS KNOW WHAT YOU WANT, AND STICK TO IT WITHOUT WAVERING. A few years ago I was going to do a degree. I had got into Wimbledon to do Fine Art, and on the first day I asked if I could make a pop video because the reason why I applied is because they said they also had good film facilities.

She said I wasn't allowed to make a pop video, but I could make a comment on one.

I was shocked by the restriction being placed on me as an artist, considering the money I was going to part with, so I left that day, not having a clue as to where my life could take me.

A big risk to some.

I felt like I had wandered out into the wilderness.

I was so disappointed and upset that I didn't do a degree, and also couldn't, as it would have been against my artistic integrity to be told that I can't do something that is artistic. So that is where my journey began for me, I decided to take stock of everything I had been taught, and to formulate a plan to become a better artist outside the system. It took sometime though. I decided to turn this into a blessing for me

Yes it was a wilderness for a bit, till ideas started forming.

So while everyone was telling me to get a proper nine to five job, and my peers were doing their degree, I was formulating a plan to create a career that suited me. I kind of knew I was on this journey, but it was a hard thing to explain to anyone, and I didn't truly understand until ideas started unfolding.

Don't let the system stagnate you, have a vision and a path, this choice will give your life purpose.

Live within your means if you want to attain your gift.

This is vital as the best ideas come when the budget is minimal.

Professional people in high positions will respect you, and you will have so much respect for yourself when you follow this path that you will have a much better sense of wellbeing. Yes there will be struggles, but the struggles will be worth it in the long run. And believe it or not, you will be a creative person living in the real world, and expressing yourself in the 'New Age of Expressive Capital'.

As you can see the artistic rebel in me that rebelled against the system, has given me my gift, and it has given me wings.

A degree would of left me upset and confused by the system, that is designed to help, but doesn't really care, or even help you to fit into this new culture that has emerged. If you know what you want, stick to it without wavering. It may take a few years, but I'm hoping my book will speed things up for you.

Alternatively you could use the ideas in this book alongside a degree.

Often for some people, doing a degree can set people back three years. For some, it helps them get to where they want to be, if you are on a degree and you want to stick with it, use some of the ideas in the book to inspire you, as it's the substance of the portfolio that matters in the end, and how you find your niche too.

ENJOY YOUR GIFT

Chapter 17

POINTS OF A COMPASS

YOUR PATH IS LIKE POINTS OF A COMPASS, ONE DEGREE OUT AND YOU WILL END UP SOMEWHERE ELSE.

You see if you take a protractor and observe the 180 degree, place it on a page, and draw a line going off in each different direction, you will notice if you veer one or even a quarter of a millimetre off, in a few miles you will end up somewhere else.

See these miles in years, if you would like to have a view of where your path could end up. It would be a long walk back to get to where you want to be, and also a good few years to get back to where you want to be.

Extraordinary but true.

your educational and personal study choices like veering off a quarter of a millimetre from your intended target using the protractor analogy. If you know what you want, and know how to get it, you will never even consider even being half or a quarter of a millimetre off course. And the way to be focused is to deal effectively with the many distractions that could come your way.

Note: Exploring your creativity is not going off your intended target, if you keep referring back to your original goal.

HOW TO APPROACH AN UNSTIMULATING EDUCATIONAL ENVIRONMENT...

If you feel you are on a course that isn't stimulating you to achieve what you want to achieve, change teachers or change college too. Or demand more from the course if you have already invested time and money and you feel it isn't right to change settings. Follow your creative prompts on this matter.

YOU FIRST HAVE TO KNOW WHAT YOU WANT TO ACHIEVE....

If you want to attain your gift, don't keep going back to the same class over and over again, unless you feel like there is something you haven't learnt before. Or the teacher can give you one to one tuition to get you onto a higher level. Or you could pay for private tuition away from a formal college.

Group lessons often stay at the same level, if you keep going back, you will get excellent at that level, but you will never move on, and expand yourself.

Keep reaching for something higher, but still get the basics under your belt first.

AIM HIGH... VERY HIGH...

If you do want to reach a higher level, taking the advice in this book in your own time will make the journey quicker. Group education is good, one to one teaching excellent, but actively participating in self education will help you have so much more to offer the group or tuition practice you are part of. If there are, safe practice, and health and safety procedures, you have to adhere to, it is advisable to learn this from a professional on a course, and then ask advice about doing this in your own time. Also with dance and sport, you need to be aware of safe bodywork practice, if you are going to practice in your own time. This prevents troublesome injuries occurring possibly in the future.

Also to prevent boredom, it's good to do a couple of intensive two week courses in your chosen activity, this helps you decide if it's the right for you, it can also stimulate inspiration, and increase your creative vocabulary. You can take the advice in this book alongside adult education if you feel you lack the creative vocabulary to achieve your goals. It's up to you to choose the right class for your level, and the level you aspire towards.

HOW TO SET UP YOUR OWN CREATIVE GROUP...

You can set up you own group on sites like Facebook and Twitter. Both can be used to advertise a blog that is associated with a group. If you have a strong idea, you will get followers. But also less time spent on social media more time for creativity. Also sharing on social media means you get feedback that can prompt you onto greater heights. Again you will make this discovery for yourself.

But you will have to have social media action plan drawn up, as a way to keep people connected into your idea. This too, will come through inspiration, and some of the ideas in this book will hopefully help you generate your own ideas for this. If the group has a lot of substance, you can get Arts Council funding if it actively gives something back to the community, or funding from other organisations if your creative project takes on a different form.

You could find people who have empty properties through an agency, so you can make use of an empty property for a lower fee, they will probably be grateful if this prevents vandalism and you get your group to take care of the building.

Helping people find their gift could be your gift, this could be just a rewarding, and in the process you could discover new skills that you never thought you had. This could be an idea for a group.

Also if you would like to set up a group, you could arrange weekly, bi-monthly, or monthly meetings in a coffee shop, pub or community centre. It would be good if it was a regular thing, and at the same location. All groups will need one or two people who are responsible for any queries, and never attend a group at someone's house, always meet in a public place. This idea is about getting like minded people connected. It's up to you how you decide on the structure and substance of your group.

WORKING IN A TEAM.

The creative path and the sporting path is often a personal one. But the more you self-achieve, with hard work and long hours by yourself, the more effective your contribution to the team will be.

 It's up to you to put the hours in and to make yourself an outstanding team member. And you can put in this effort during personal time and team time, so the two can blend beautifully. And as we all have a gift, and if you follow your inspiring prompts to find your gift, you will find it. And if you work hard, be persistent, your contribution to society and to the community with your wonderful gift will be tremendous.

Also, it isn't all just about physical skills; it is about emotional skills too, though this book does focus on attaining a physical skill that can be measured.

And in the age of machinery, it's the social skills that are being treasured the most because that's what makes us human. An essential part of developing your gift, is nurturing your social and personal skills too. Because remember, they are not just buying into your gift, they are also buying into you.

Being well rounded will make you and the gift you have an indispensible part of this culture we now live in.

Chapter 18

CREATING EFFECTIVE PROMPTS

So you've done your studying and received your knowledge, and in this process you've chosen your gift subject. Mine was drawing, yours could be anything. Just to say, that the purpose of attaining this knowledge, is so that you have information with which you can be creative with. This automatically turns you into an artist.

Using knowledge in a creative way is artistry; you have started to become original.

Well if you have trouble getting prompts, don't worry, reread my book, or go to a favourite place, or listen to a meditation tape you have an affinity towards. Or anything else you do to help you create prompts.

Remember I said relevant knowledge creates inspiration, and also some people do have this inner spirit where they have an ability to acquire their gift, and a market for this too.

I call this instinct.

In some ways they are lucky.

But I guess I created this idea, as some people do have to go through a slower more thoughtful process, and I wanted to be able to break it down into independent, manageable steps. I feel I have achieved this, and there is more on this towards the end of this book. My book isn't just about creating your gift; it's about being free of the constraints that hold us back in life. If you want to look at these ideas in more depth, ask the Universe, and you will be shown literature and ideas and people that will give you more information than I can cover. Focus is the key, and I have chosen to focus on 'How to Develop Your Gift'. And within this it is also about how to choose your gift too.

I also wrote this book as I wish I had read a book like this years ago and I also noticed there wasn't one like this on the market. If you enjoy it then fabulous, if not then you would of at least gained an opinion that will be valuable to you and your creative journey.

Also the thing with being creative, when you have a fabulous idea, you have to be strict on yourself. You have to commit yourself and put the other ideas in a folder for later, or as a reminder of an idea you could have used but decided not to. By focusing and committing to an idea, when you do get a creative prompt, you know it's a prompt to head you in the right direction. Even though this idea is great, I still get fluffy ideas that pop into my head, but as this idea strengthens itself, I know what to adhere to, and what is a silly idea.

GIVE YOUR DREAM TO YOUR IMAGINATION

My creative imagination is full of brilliant ideas and very silly ideas, and it's all cool and fun. I suppose if I just had great ideas all the time, I would become very egotistical, the silly ideas keep me grounded.

And also, the trick about giving your dream to your imagination is that it is like breathing, you just do it naturally.

Being able to create your own creative prompts and respond in a way that brings creative substance, is far cheaper than these very expensive degrees. Self- attained is so much better than spoon fed education, and you can work alongside a brilliant teacher on a one to one level using this self-attainment technique I have talked about, and still to talk about in further parts of this book.

ENJOY YOUR GIFT

Chapter 19

WHAT TO DO IF YOU ALREADY HAVE YOUR GIFT

You may have university, or just completed a Masters, just finished and you are wondering what to do next. You may have an exquisite talent that you acquired through privately paid tuition or even by yourself, or through inspiration. I'm not sure where you are at; it's up to you to decide. Even if you're content with your gift, there is always going to be times when you need a nudge in a higher direction.

So you may be fed up of studying, and need a break, if you do, do that, it will be an important time for you, to recharge your batteries after being brainwashed by the system. When you have reignited your passion for knowledge, start to study, and gain knowledge. As I have explained in the earlier part of this book and still in the later part of this book. Gain knowledge that you feel is relevant to your path you are now on, or a new path you would like to be on. Go beyond what these colleges have taught you, rise above them. Find out more about what is happening in the real world. If you did a degree in Fine Art, ask yourself, 'Do I really want to spend the rest of my life making comments on things, could there be another way?' Swot analyse what you have learnt at university or privately and compare it with what's happening now.

Just to note, I have alter reignited my passion for fine art at a recent exhibition about endangered animals and here I could see the value of making comments as it is a subject that is close to my heart. One that stood out was a tiger skin the same colour as grass; this idea spoke volumes to me.

Have a plan. Don't take the first dead end job that is offered to you. Now that you are reading this book, you are on a mission. If you are a classical musician, study the ones who did something different with their talent, and do something different yourself.

Try not to copy them, that is not being original, aspire towards them, but don't copy their format.

If you enjoy playing in an orchestra, do this, but market yourself in such a way that you are indispensible to the classical music scene. This is something you have to figure out for yourself, and you do this by following creative prompts.

ENJOY YOUR GIFT

Chapter 20

COPYING IS CREATIVE, IF DONE IN A UNIQUE WAY

COPYING IS CREATIVE IF DONE IN A UNIQUE WAY. We all learn by copying. If you love a dance company watch the company on YouTube, or at the local theatre and research other dance companies in a similar vein. Copy the moves in your own way or exactly. Do this safely by warming up first. Even take some dance training before you decide to get creative. It's fun and inspiring to copy. But if you really want to improve your dancing skill, read about the history of dance and it's development and take notes. This will make your dance classes more informed. You don't have to wait till you are on a formal course to do this, you can do this now. By all means share with the teacher, if she has some time before or after the class, if not just keep it to yourself, like minded people will turn up and you can share your discoveries with them instead. And too, you will develop your own style of dancing by choosing to study a variety of dance styles, and from this you can invent your own.

Singers copy before they find their own voice, some have their own voice straight away.

Always train your voice safely and never strain the vocal chords.

If you copy directly too much, you will end up mimicking, this can be a good thing if used creatively, but not a good thing if you want to be a truly unique artist.

So artists copy the Greats, singers copy great singers, dancers copy great dancers, musicians copy great musicians. Do this safely and sensibly and seek professional mentors to guide you to do this safely especially with vocals as using your vocal chords safely and correctly means you take care of your instrument for life.

This is all good.

But to be truly unique, copy, then go your own way. Copying expressively will help you create in a new and unique way.

Good one to one teachers can get you out of the habit of direct copying. You can do this yourself to by looking at your art, or doing a play back of your dance music and singing. I did singing lessons for ages before I recorded myself. You need to know how you sound when singing, and what you look like when dancing. This applies to acting and sport too

WRITING SO MY WORDS ARE EFFECTIVE.

I have deliberately chosen not to put in words that are unfamiliar, because getting up to look in a dictionary can ruin the flow of my message.

The message is to change society, by getting people to think and act for themselves regarding their gift.

Some people prefer to work with, and read challenging words because they love the English language, but I want to master the simple notes first. I want to be more like an experienced chef with my words, creating something exquisite with the simplest ingredients that most people have heard of before. Like a beautiful simple recipe, that tastes, smells, and looks out of this world. My ideas are not new; they are just put together in a unique and original way.

And that's what I'm delivering to you, simplicity with brains, it's always effective.

YOUR CREATIVE IMAGINATION IS YOUR FRIEND.

Always trust that your creative imagination is showing you the right path. It will drive you, show you, give you, anything you believe to be possible. It is the creative side of God. The imagination is the creative side of God. God is your friend.

Focusing on what you want regarding your gift, will bring you what you want regarding your gift.

And your creative imagination is the powerhouse of your desire regarding this. **This is the creative side of God**

THE EMPEROR IS NAKED.

The Emperor is running the system and he is naked, and no one has the guts to say anything, apart from one person whose notion of reality is to see things as they really are.

But we have got better things to do than observe the obvious. If we choose to ignore the obvious, it's not because of our ignorance, but because we have got better things to do with our precious time.

Ironically, by taking advice like this and other advice, we are doing more than ignoring, we are moving in a positive direction.

Laughing at the Emperor would be a waste of time, and I've kind of done it for you in this book.

You get on with your duty to the kingdom of creativity, to discover your gift. Because my work is about creating a new way, apart from the system, and for humours sake I will call it, 'Entering the kingdom of true creativity'.

It's ok to laugh, because I'm sure the system has laughed at us by treating us like we are stupid at times. And we are not. We were just afraid of our own genius, but not anymore.

ENJOY YOUR GIFT

Chapter 21

SEEING CREATIVITY AS A SCIENCE

There is a science behind this order that I have chosen to write in. It's written too in a similar way to a diary writer writes, as my idea has unfolded, I've kept the exact same order, I feel that the order is correct for me, but you can also dip into each of the parts as and when you wish too. This idea may not work for everyone, it won't work for everyone, as we are all different, and we all have our own unique approach to creativity.

I guess I wanted to be like a scientist who could unlock the mystery of creativity with a provable method. One I proved on myself. An also through publishing this book I will find out what works for others too.

My previous work does show the remarkable improvement that I have made and without teacher intervention.

You could argue it could have happened anyway. But that's not the point; I've shared with you how I changed my life. And you can use this work to make a summary of all of your talents, and your life's work.

Everyone's story will be different, and following my idea could be a good thing. But this book is also about you getting onto your own personal creative path.

When you study, often you are doing something you don't want to do, because you know that doing it will help you get onto the next level, the level you prefer. Some courses that I hated doing, I did anyway, because I like to follow through on things and get to the next level. You could create your own science around your own personal path to creativity.

The path is up to you.

Use your own inventiveness to make your own discoveries.

THE IMPORTANCE OF VISUAL THINKING……

Even if no one understands your drawing, the fact that you do, is a start. You have taken this incredible step to free yourself from this cog-drone thinking, and you are now a unique creative individual in your own right.

I don't know where this path is going to take you, and also neither do you, that is why it's exciting. You are now able to put your vision down on paper, and that is an incredible skill to have. You have the ability to communicate your own ideas, not surplus ideas spoon fed to you by the system.

This skill will be invaluable to you no end.

Your drawings are not part of the system or a spoon fed class, your drawings are you, and this is your voice.

Now you have your voice, you can figure it out for yourself, where you want to take your art.

I can't tell you that, I can only advise you for the first year of this project. The rest is up to you.

I am currently working on the next part of this project, but this will take time, and perhaps I can advise you on the next stage, but in the meantime you can figure out the next stage for yourself. I'm not here to create a new system. I'm here to help you get onto the right path, to help you think for yourself. The rest is up to you. It could take you a year, or longer, it's taken me most of my life. If this idea is a shortcut for you, fabulous, just remember it took me much longer. And too, some people don't need to read a book like this because they just know. We are all different, that's life.

ENJOY YOUR GIFT

Chapter 22

THE CULTURE OF GIFT GIVING

Five hundred years ago, before the institutionalisation of money and the legalisation of usury (paying interest on loans) we had tribes. Within these tribes there was a gift system, that's why capitalism has always slated because it didn't always exist. This gift system meant that the most powerful in the tribe would give gifts. Capitalism turned this on its head, and now for the past five hundred years we have a culture of, 'I pay you for this, and return you give me the exact value of what I pay you' with the receiver of the money making a profit.

And since then, we have a culture where the most powerful one is the receiver of gifts.

Now with the new global market that we live in, in order to get noticed we must give gifts. You do this with social media updates.

TREAT YOUR SOCIAL MEDIA UPDATES AS A GIFT YOU ARE GIVING...

These gifts have now changed, it's now a link to something, or information that is useful to the recipient.

It is a form of social interaction that we crave, and the fact that it's free, really brings back what a true notion of what a gift is.

If someone wants something and the other wants something in return, it can either be seen as a social contract or a form of manipulation. But really if someone wants something in return, it's not truly a gift. Sometimes the giving and receiving of gifts is expected too.

Where is the joy in that, if something is demanded in return?

DEVELOPING YOUR GIFT AND GIVING YOUR GIFT.

So with this talent you are developing, in order to communicate it effectively in this global age, you need to know how to develop your gift, and give a gift at the same time.

When you start to do your work from this point of view, everything will change for you.

And that's what I mean by following hunches, we have a desire to go back to our tribal way of living, before the culture of trade and commerce changed the face of the world forever with capitalism.

It's just we have to blend the culture of gift giving, with the culture of capitalism, without leaving yourself out of pocket.

STANDING OUT AND THE NEW RULES.

The new rules mean that our ancestry, our birth, our hereditary, will not guarantee success. Success is up to you.

If you are wealthy you cannot get your butler to read this book for you and do the exercises, you have to do it for yourself, diligently.

If you are a boss or an entrepreneur or a business owner, can you take six months out of your business where you can read for three months and exploring drawing for three months? If you could, and you are following hunches, you could improve your business no end if you feel this book is anyway relevant to you.

You won't lose six months if you have a plan, you will only gain.

If you ask someone else to do this for you, you could lose out. You could take it in turns, but personally I do think it's a good idea if the boss does this first. Do you want your business to stand out? If you do, you need to take these steps to invest your time. It's a method, and if you follow it in your own personal way, it could make ideas come to you that will surprise you forever. You could alternate between reading art books and business books for three months and doing drawing. This work is all a good foundation for creating an inventive blog about your line of creativity.

You need to research and take action, if you want to be a success and stand out among the masses.

If you don't have time to read this book and do the exercises, you could read a book called 'Making Ideas Happen' by Scott Belsky.

This will help you with ideas and team building.

YOU HAVE TO REMEMBER THAT THERE IS A BIG DIFFERENCE BETWEEN HAVING AN IDEA AND ATTAINING YOUR GIFT...

KEEP RESPONDING TO CREATIVE PROMPTS...

Resistance is useless. I was going to write resistance is futile, but even I had to look up futile in the dictionary, and I thought it could be phrase that belonged to someone else, and after all this book is an exercise in creative writing as well as ideas. I thought it meant pointless, but it means useless, similar.

But in the game of creativity, you need to be precise, sometimes…….

I could have decided not to write that, and given in to the resistance. But I feel the human touch is going to make this writing successful. If you respond and keep responding, creativity will flow, and you won't need to worry about resistance. Yes it's good to be aware of what holds us back, but focusing on it will hold us back even further.

YOU HAVE TO TAKE ACTION, PURPOSEFUL ACTION…

Focus on the positive, and what's possible.

That's why I keep talking about inner creative prompts, like your own personal inner teacher or guide.

Focus on that, practice responding to these creative prompts, and you will go down such interesting paths and life will become extraordinary, and you will be like a breath of fresh air. Then if you focus on what you want, criticism will flow off you like water off a ducks back. Sod the resistance, you are creative, and you are following and responding to your prompts.

ENJOY YOUR GIFT

Chapter 23

RACHAELS DREAM VERSES THE AMERICAN DREAM

With the American dream, it made us believe that there was room for everyone, and it broke a lot of hearts.

But in truth, it spat a lot of people out, and welcomed others wholeheartedly, and we couldn't work out why.

And the people who got spat out were nauseously told that the reason why they got spat out is because 'They didn't believe'.

And it felt like a smack in the face with a frozen kipper.

It wasn't what we expected, but for some, it was the reality of what happened. Well, you do have to believe, but we no longer have to believe in the American Dream (a product of the industrial age) because the American Dream isn't working anymore. We are now living in a new culture 'The Culture of the Gift', and for humour's sake I will call it 'Rachael's Dream'.

My dream spits out the system, and helps those creative's flourish, and the one's that never fitted in. Now people, who felt they never had a place in the American dream, can build their own dream. Yes it will cost you around nine months, to a year to get started, but this will get you onto a sure footing, to help you find your own path. It did me, and it can for you too. So this work will help you spit out the system, and replace it with Susan's Dream, Steven Dream, Harry's Dream, Sarah's Dream, and anyone who dares to dream a dream's, dream. Just as long as it isn't the American Dream, we will be ok and happy.

This is anyone's dream, and there is no one who isn't welcome, except those that want to mechanise my idea and turn it into a system. And those that are so far in trenched in the system that they have become creative vultures, they are not welcome.

It's not a system, and it never will be a system. You see, I'm interested in creating a tribe, as I said before, a tribe of people who will give this creative path a go, a take a risk, just like I did, and see what will happen. Call it a vision, call it what you like, but I'm an action lady, and I like things to happen.

Otherwise life gets boring and we can't have that can we.

Focus on that, practice responding to these creative prompts, and you will go down such interesting paths and life will become extraordinary, and you will be like a breath of fresh air. Then if you focus on what you want, criticism will flow off you like water off a ducks back. Sod the resistance, you are creative, and you are following and responding to your prompts.

ROCKING THE STATUS QUO...

Having no attachment to the outcome, and only a desire to respond to prompts, regarding the gift project, you are now on, will rock the status quo.

Everyone is worrying. The design of this idea is so you don't have to worry. The system wants us to worry, this idea cannot fail you, and it's free, and you will receive something, at least the experience of having tried. I followed through, so can you.

THE FUTURE IS NOT SOLID...

Don't visualise the future in terms of a solid outcome, just step by step, day by day, respond to these prompts. By all means have a vision, but let it grow, flow, and develop. If it's a fixed dream, by all means go for it. But if you have a fixed idea to an outcome of the idea, or goal, you may miss opportunities that are vital.

Let go of the outcome, and the paths you walk will surprise you, and bring you joy beyond measure. And did you notice I said this idea is a design, with steps on how to do it in your own way, to make it your own design. How many books show you how to do something for yourself, that is different from the author's outcome? So, when you have designed your gift, and arrived, you can show others how to do the same, and this is how you create a new community.

This will be your tribe. This could also be my own tribe, as I get the people who show interest, interested in following through. I'm not sure what will happen, all I know is that I enjoy this path, and I plan to stay on it and see where else I will end up

ENJOY YOUR GIFT

Chapter 24

DISCERNING THE DIFFERENCE

You will, when you start to share, discern the difference between positive feedback and damaging criticism. You may think it would be easy to do, but often comments can be underhand and mixed with charming compliments. Don't listen to the creative vultures, unless it is to bounce off them. I have created some of my best work when I have reacted against creative vultures.

And in this bouncing, can help refine and define your mission. Avoid them if possible, it's just they suck out your creative juices, the way a vampire sucks blood.

Just visualise water flowing off a ducks back, and go on your way. If you are inexperienced with your goal, life is long, just enjoy the journey. Life is full of surprises, never give up.

One day the people who where underhand with you, will wish they had been more encouraging, when you finally succeed.

ALWAYS ASPIRE TO THE GREATS...

As scientist of creativity, who conducted the experiment on herself, to create these illustrations, I could suggest that you do this idea in a different order perhaps, a month of reading, a month of drawing, till it makes up 6 to 9 months of study.

It could work and suit some people a lot more.

But what I am saying is, once you take an average drawer to a very good drawer using this technique, you can't redo it at this level on the same person. It's been done on the person at this level. If this way is preferable then do this, but don't expect the same results. You will get a result if the intention is there. But I still believe that a good three months solid of reading is the best bet, as it gives you a stronger foundation to do things. Remember, when you are reading, you are learning how the Greats drew, this means you get ideas and drawing advice from these books, something that is unique to your journey, and the style of art you aspire too. Again this can be applied to any skill. Also don't forget to draw from the famous masters too, as I did this a lot before I embarked on the reading side of things.

That's why I'm not teaching you how to draw. I want you to learn from the Greats. Ok you can learn from people at my level, I'm not saying I've nothing to give, I'm saying this to you, so you can create higher ambitions, by aspiring to the Greats, that's how society progresses. But you can also look at my recent work and see if anything inspires you as it has improved immensely. I will keep drawing so if you keep looking at my page you will see something there that you enjoy, but remember I am doing it for me so if you don't enjoy it I wont worry.

WRITER'S BLOCK...

This method could be used to combat writers block, visual thinking is a useful tool to release words that need releasing. I wrote his book from my passion and I didn't experience writers block at all.

All writers need to do research, and writers block could be simply that you are writing for the masses and not from your passion.

Also, reading books for leisure while writing can inspire ideas too.

Follow your prompts, it may even mean you try a different creative path for a while, to inspire your writing a few years down the line.

If you start drawing, you could research writers that have combined drawing and art together in their writing. Look at 'The Little Prince' by Antoine De Saint-Exupery; this is a perfectly charming example of creative writing, and beautiful illustrations that blend perfectly.

Following this advice could help you find something to write about too. Even if it's writing about how you tried out this idea for a year.

There is no such thing as writers block anyway, not anymore. Writers block just means that you need to do something else for a while. Beautiful eh!

RESUME OR GIFT.

Creating a gift portfolio...

How I see it is, that the creative path, if you have used it intelligently, you will have something to show for it. I am aware that there are sites where people do network and get work in artistic fields. But do employers go direct to them when looking for employees.

What I am suggesting is that we could go about creating Gift Portfolio's with the aim to getting work. These can be a blog or a website or a fan page, or even a new type of website could be created that isn't just for networking, but is more direct in getting work in creative fields, instead of the opportunities just going to in house applicants.

Having a strong gift portfolio could enhance your CV and even be an alternative to a CV.

Too, if someone has a Gift Portfolio, it will show picture of people actually on the job, so this would cut out people blagging for work on CV's. A blog shows who you are, and what you can do, while you are doing it. An idea too, that could stamp out bogus professionals in many fields not just art, maybe in medicine and animal professions too. Showing a blog on a laptop of your skills in action would be a perfect tool for a job interview.

There is a network called the Behance Network for artists and illustrators, I've heard it very good, and there is also Pinterest and Instagram too.

ATLANTIS AND THE END OF THE WORLD...

The problem with Great art these days is, either we have run out of affordable land, or we just use the land to make huge amounts of money. The fear seems, that we feel that it is either going to be swallowed up by the sea like Atlantis, or God's Wrath will burn it to the ground.

So we have stopped creating brilliance (this debate is open to opinion) and we have shied away from Great Art in this fear. And we have reduced ourselves to making timid or monstrous art that has outstanding opinions and ideas attached to it, but no beauty.

Our voice is out there loud and clear, but our true skills have disappeared, (like Atlantis).

The more clever the message, the less outstanding contemporary art feel it needs to be. We think we are free, but we are not.

Fine art is still controlled by the system, the consensus, and the colleges still control the content too.

We need to create beautiful art again, and let it speak for itself. Perhaps one day it will again, hopefully. But ok all art is beautiful, but I am just writing this to challenge you and make you think.

Chapter 25

ART IS ABOUT INSPIRING CHANGE, TOO

Art isn't all about having a voice, making comments, and saying what you think, it's about inspiring change. Maybe I will create these illustrations in this way for the rest of my life, maybe I will decide to embark on another project. At the time of writing this book I was going through a discovery process and I wrote a book to share this process with you.

Anyway this book isn't about me, and the way I choose to live my life, it's about you, and you not wasting your time, talent, and opportunity.

What will our culture think of us in a 1000 year's time, or even 2000 years? Is the world really going to end? What if it didn't? Are we still going to dot the landscape with ugly monstrosities, or are we going to leave something so breathtakingly beautiful for our ancestors to admire?

Our freedom of speech is loud and clear, but the voice and the talent is somehow separated.

Stonemasons are no longer artists they have become crafts people, just in the business of restoration. Can we not afford genius anymore, has the money run out, are we so stuck, that we are afraid to do something for future generations, possibly in 1000 or 2000 years time?

All we have dotting our landscapes, are pretend beautiful buildings that pay homage to the industrial age.

We are Post Industrial, and we don't need to be reminded of this recent past.

Let's go back 2000 years, before we even think about going forward.

We must stop and think before we create, and ask ourselves why are we creating in the first place?

ENJOY YOUR GIFT

Chapter 26

WRITE YOUR OWN BOOK

WRITE YOUR OWN BOOK ABOUT YOUR GIFT AND HOW YOU ACHIEVED IT, AND THEN TURN IT INTO A BLOG OR A BOOK ON AMAZON.

I created my gift using my method, and then I wrote this book. Solid hard work that was what it was.

I did do a lot of research too, on how to give my message more substance, by reading lots of book around my area of interest. It's good to share and that's how we connect and grow, and create ideas for new and better ideas. I'm just really looking forward to completing this book, so I can go back into my drawing.

This writing is really a platform for future projects.

By people understanding my thinking, and understanding the way I work, will make it a lot more easier and simpler to communicate how I plan to approach future projects.

Communication is the key, and by writing this, I make things clearer.

I may remain a solo creative, or I may decide to do create something with a team.

Either way this book is a good foundation for any path I choose to take. This book gives me the freedom to open doors that need opening, in more ways than one. It can do the same for you too.

START WITH THE IDEA OF THE GIFT.

And, it is in the giving and sharing of your gift, that you will attain further ideas on how to push your gift into new dimensions. It's done this for me; it can do it for you too.

Sharing is the new culture.

As you are developing your gift, think about how you are going to share it. I don't understand how this works it just does. Sharing is the new creating, providing you share and create at the right time. It's worked for me, and it's worked for countless others too.

If you think about how you will share your talent, the gift and brilliant ideas will emerge.

THE GOAL IS NOT TO STANDARDISE THE GIFT.

As you are exploring your gesture drawing, scales, chords, body conditioning, and any other gift attaining technique, remember you are still exploring. Yes there is an element where one desires perfection, but remember it is in the exploration that you will find beauty. Yes, persue the line, or the note, or the muscle definition and alignment, till it is perfect, but you must remember that perfection is not the goal. Applying the technique in the best possible way is the goal. Perfection is just a by-product of the exploration.

You limit yourself by trying to achieve perfection straight away. Perfection should be a surprise, not the goal. You raise the bar when you explore. Explore the scales, the chords, the drawing, the body conditioning, don't just do it, keep exploring.

This idea is game changing, and it is also non linear, as you can take it to where ever it wants to go.

Learn these rules and explore your findings, and share your findings with people who want the best for you, those who can bring you up to greater heights.

Also if you feel like you have reached perfection, raise the bar further by continuing to explore, and there will be new levels of perfection that will be open to you. Perfection is never perfect; there is always new levels to aspire towards. Explore to reach perfection.

Also with this exploring, you have to learn to be inspired by unfinished pieces of your own work, which is the art, or music explored.

You have to imagine how it can become better and believe that with each create step you take daily, it is bringing you closer to your goals. When things start to come together beautifully, you will appreciate every hour and every minute that you took to explore. Exploring is the way to perfection. And with continued exploring you will reach new levels of perfection that you never even knew existed. By your continued exploring, you will reach new territories with your art music and dance, and in this way your life's work will never be standardised. Exploring is the lifetime ambition. By all means do what works for you, but explore what works for you, and take what works for you to new levels, and beyond your own area of experience and expertise.

BUY ELEGANT STYLISH SKETCHBOOK TO WORK IN AT THE LATER STAGES.

Ok these you can get for around a few pounds more than the standard sketchbooks, and you could consolidate all of you best ideas into a few neat elegant sketchbooks that you can refer back too at a later date.

You need to have a system so you can review all of your work.

If you sell any work, always take photos/scans first, and log the photo/scans into an organised file with a date. Try to keep all of your work in date order, so you can closely monitor your progress. Keep all work neat in a folder, even if you don't like it very much. This is useful in case you want to blog the results of your effort. By keeping sketchbooks neatly, you end up with a stronger conviction of where your talents lie.

Remember also, a business mentor is not an artist, he can only advise you on business. Unless you show these sketchbooks to your business mentor, he will never really understand how you think as a creative individual, and still then, he may not understand you.

These sketchbooks, especially one's created outside formal education, will show you a lot about who you are as an artist, your goals, your ideas, and which ideas to keep and which ideas to reject. If you learn to consolidate your ideas, these sketchbooks can be like your mentors.

Even sports people and dancers should keep sketchbooks, as being able to think visually can inform your physical skills, and help define your goals a lot more clearly.

Tom Daley the Olympic Diver drew a picture of him winning the Olympics age 10 and a few years later he did.

ENJOY YOUR GIFT

Chapter 27

THE CLEVERNESS BEHIND YOUR UNIQUENESS

THE CLEVERNESS BEHIND YOUR UNIQUENESS AND EMOTIONAL LABOUR AND PHYSICAL LABOUR...

Although this sounds very unromantic, because some people do believe artists do create out of the ethereal, we do have to put emotional and physical labour into our work. While emotional labour in isolation does mean our effort and our personality as well as body language too.

When you are attaining your gift, if you are doing it for an audience later down the line, invest in emotional and physical labour combined. This is what will give your work a unique essence. It is the emotional effort manifesting itself in the physical that will bring you the results that you desire. You capture your audience much more, by investing in your own personal version of emotional labour, combined with your talent.

Ironically, sometimes, it's the singer with less technical capabilities that puts in genuine emotion that can move an audience to tears.

Yet technical expertise still is appreciated and something to be aimed for.

If you already have the technical expertise, try putting more emotion into your work and see what happens...

Always do both anyway, the more you practice, the more the combination of physical and emotional labour will come naturally to you, and show up in you work.

ENJOY YOUR GIFT

Chapter 28

THE IMPORTANCE OF JOY

AND IN PUTTING MORE EMOTION INTO YOUR WORK YOU WILL EXPERIENCE JOY.
The joy of connecting with people: your audience, and also the audience that you don't see, via print and digital sales.

Bob Dylan, put emotion into his work, he wasn't interested in mass media culture, and his influences were certainly not mass media icons. He was reputed to refuse to go electric at a concert, preferring acoustic because he felt that this was the best medium to play to his audience. He was true to his subject and he became a legend in doing so.

He told the truth about his art and stuck by what he believed.

His path may not be your path, be true to yourself, and not necessarily copy someone who was true to their path; unless you feel it is the right path for you. Being true to your subject isn't an easy thing to do. Yes there will be struggles, but you will experience the joy of knowing that you were true to yourself and your goals. Also by following creative prompts, you will gain creative control of your work, and hopefully not get sucked into another system of mass media control.

Try to keep your own creative control. The point of this book is for you to gain artistic freedom, and for you to be true to your beliefs. If having a record company in charge of your art, gives you the creative freedom you desire, by all means sign up. But remember, a contract is a contract and you could become a cog in its system too, without realising. Just find a contract that allows you creativity. This could make you end up on a creative path that no longer inspires you, genuinely from the depths of your soul. Don't seek celebrity status just for the sake of it, be smart, be true, and seek a path that brings you joy. It may be the path you least expect, life is like that sometimes.

ENJOY YOUR GIFT

Chapter 29

THE EDGES OF THE BOX

'THINKING ALONG THE EDGES OF THE BOX' INSTEAD.

Seth Godin in his book Linchpin, talks about not thinking too far outside the box because outside the box is a vacuum, and there is nothing to work against.

He says 'Think along the edges of the box', as that is where the audience is.

And on reflection, I guess I started to think along the edges of the box by deciding to draw precisely in my own way from fashion photographs. I was working on something, and against something I was told that I couldn't do, and I succeeded.

Maybe if things are not happening in your life, it is because you are not bending the rules enough.

FOCUS ON THE OPPORTUNITY YOU HAVE AT HAND...

I had an opportunity to draw from fashion photographs and I took it. It was the opportunity that was at hand. Responding to an opportunity that is available to you is often the best option. Many great advisors will tell you this, mine was drawing, yours could be anything, and it could also the opportunities suggested in this book. When you focus on this opportunity, the one you have at hand, focus on it, push it into its fruition, but remember ideas can metaphorically blow up like a meteorite entering the earth's atmosphere, learn from this, and then move onto the next inspiring opportunity. Although I was relaxed doing my illustrations, I still did them fast, not fast in a clumsy way, I just had a certain mementom, because I was eager to go onto the next project.

GIFT ENERGY LIKES SPEED...

The gift energy likes speed. Keep the energy flowing, and wonderful things will happen for you.

Keep pushing against something, i.e. the system, what you've been taught, and what you've been told is the ideal career for you.

Follow your own path, and magical things will happen, and you will become part of the forward thinking crew who are going somewhere.

ENJOY YOUR GIFT

Chapter 30

MANAGING CONFLICT AND THE LOSS OF IDEAS

As I said before, we have to be aware that some ideas do burn up, and the life of an idea is over or at least put on hold till later. And in order to manage our creative path, we have to be able to recognise this, and move onto the next project if necessary.

Many ideas are explored and never fulfilled, and some may see this as a failure. But creative's don't believe in failure, not in this sense of the word, because somehow everything, every experience somehow becomes relevant.

It's with these struggles that can sometimes feel like disappointments, that we have to manage the reactions of others, and still persist in the face of lost ideas. A lost idea can at times feel similar to a lost relationship. And yes, you can sometimes feel the same pain of a breakup from an idea, or even a failed course, just like when you have a breakup from a relationship.

But remember all those relationships that never worked out, well, when we let go, something or someone better turned up.

We can toss, turn, worry, and agonise about whether to return to an idea. But if you are following your prompts, you will cease all this agonising, and let go and allow other ideas to enter your creative mind. And remember it's sometimes when you've hit on a brilliant idea, that you meet the most resistance and conflict. Find a way to pull through, I did, I pulled through and my life is amazing now. For some people though, especially creative people, conflict fires us up and reinforces the reasons why we were pursuing the idea in the first place.

THE STEADY LIFE IS THE ARTISTIC LIFE.

When you start to confront the system you are participating in change. It will be a rocky path, to start following through, and shipping your idea to your target market, but it is this shipping that will bring you the ultimate satisfaction. Shipping your idea could be writing a project and applying for funding or responding to creative call outs.

And if it doesn't work out how you expected, you can always try again till it does work out.

The fact that you tried, took action, and gained knowledge by reading, will always be advantageous to you, no matter what.

Remember, a lot of stuff that is taught to us in the system can either be useful in the attainment of your gift, or it can be toxic. And sometimes it's the things that you learnt at school that you can reflect upon and shuffle around and use to figure out your genius. Mine was during an RE cover class. The teacher told us to rewrite our worst page and to do this very neatly and very well. During this activity the teacher took hold of my work and said very loudly in front of the whole class 'Look this isn't your worst page' and he showed me all of my worst pages, which I thought were ok, and said I should redo these. I had actually redone my best and neatest page because I wanted to make my best page neater and better. I'm quite sure I just ignored him and carried on perfecting my best page, he would of made himself look stupid if he told me off twice. I was only twelve, and already had my own mind, cool eh. School is a product of the industrial revolution, so we are just taught to do as we are told so we can get a job one day, and if you notice it isn't always the one who do as they are told who make it in life.

So the artist in me rebelled, but it wasn't rebellion, I just did what made sense to me. Doing what makes sense to you, always works in the long run, it may take time, but it will be worth it in the end.

Another thing I learnt around that time is gridding in maths. I now use this skill to square up my illustrations to the nearest half millimetre. It's not all bad we just have to be selective. Lucky I decide to redo my maths page till it was perfect, in this class the teacher never minded. Anyway sometimes not listening and doing the opposite of what is required, is a lesson we look back on to learn the greatest lesson. Later I went back into more expressive work, but this was where I was at when I first wrote this.

Perfecting what is the best page will pay off in the end. Aim for perfection whatever the cost. And when you reach perfection, explore, so that you can reach new levels of perfection. Because perfection is never perfect and you explore to reach perfection. What I am saying is, by taking your own path, and by doing your own thing creatively, this will bring you security in the end. It's just it will be a little rocky a first.

The new culture now welcomes us so much more than the American Dream once did a few years ago. We are no longer idealists, because we have figured out our mission and we are actively taking steps to fulfil our mission, and we are sharing and creating with people who matter.

Ok, some days I wasn't fired up, I just plodded along no matter how hard it was, until everything came together beautifully. So whether you are plodding along, or totally fired up, keep going as it will all come together eventually. It's nice to plod along sometimes, being fired up can be exhausting, especially if this is a lifelong ambition, pace yourself, and use that fired up energy where necessary

ENJOY YOUR GIFT

Chapter 31

KNOW WHAT YOUR WORTH IS

DEALING WITH PEOPLE WHO WANT YOUR TIME FOR FREE... You have to know your worth, or else you will be bled dry by people who show no value for your artistic skills.

You are not a charity. But working for a charity is a valuable thing.

If your idea takes off, there will be a lot of people wanting your time for nothing, be on the alert. If you have an instinct that they may not pay you when they have promised, listen to this instinct, it could well be true. You are better off doing part time work where you know you are going to get paid, then to give away your artistic talents for nothing. Working for nothing could cause resentment and take away the passion you have for your dreams.

Work towards getting paid for your talent, this is called knowing your worth. But there are times when you will have to part with time and skills for free to get this paid work, just be savvy and selective.

And if you are following the advice in this book, and following through, you won't have time to work for free. Also ideas are not free. Don't willingly give away ideas that you have slavishly developed and considered, if there isn't going to be a reward or a paper trail that leads back to you. OK, so there are times when sharing an idea is purposeful. You just have to respond to your instincts to work out if it is right to do so.

I once told a market research company to use all six ideas for their Christmas advertising campaign as they were all good. It was a focus group for Argos Christmas Campaign; they used my idea to use all six advertisements. The purpose of the focus group was to get the public to choose one. Ok, they may of made a lot of money from my idea to use all six ideas, but how I saw it was that, when I work from home, and I have the TV on in the background, at least I don't have to see an advert repeated a hundred times. I now get variety, and the idea has caught on, all the advertising campaigns do this now.

ENJOY YOUR GIFT

Chapter 32

CREATE YOUR OWN DESTINY

REMEMEMBER THE SYSTEM IS A MAP AND WE ARE NO LONGER OBEYING THIS MAP BUT CREATING OUR OWN DESTINIES...

Well there will always be things that we will have to do because we love to fit in, that's life, and it can be good sometimes. Anyway the artistic life isn't so rebellious now. It will soon be the norm to follow our own maps and create our own destinies.

You are being a leader now, a leader on a mission, and new tribes are all getting together, and embracing this new life, and everything is cool.

But hey, in life no matter what, we will always have resistance. This is good, as this can give us something to fight against. And fighting against something isn't always negative. It just depends on how we do it. One way to do this is to be inspired, anxiety cannot tolerate inspiration, neither can the resistance.

Once you are inspired you are existing in a spiritual realm, although your feet are on the ground. Do make sure that during this time, that you are inspired, that you are grounded, otherwise you may not take those vital steps to achieve your goals.

And when you are inspired, you are living by your own rules, and your life is amazing, and no one really understands you, and you don't really care. Because you trust that everything will work out just fine. But there will come a time when you want people to understand you, but you do it because you need others to understand the insights that you have discovered along the way.

It is innate in our human psyche, part of our story telling tradition that has been with us for thousands of years, to go off on an adventure, and comeback to the tribe and tell them all about what you have learnt. Maybe I've inspired you to create your own story, for you to go off on your creative travels, and later write a story or a blog. If you do, make sure it is a good story one worth reading and learning from.

IS IT PURPOSEFUL OR POINTLESS?

Purposeful and pointless distractions.....

There is a fine line between the purposeful and the pointless when it comes to creativity. If you are creative through and through, nothing is pointless, but you do have to reign in your creative schedule so that you are being purposely productive.

PASSION and **FOCUS** will make your pointless distractions purposeful.

We all get distracted don't we? It's just how we use it creatively that will make our endeavours productive.

USING YOUR OWN HANDWRITTING DURING YOUR GIFT DEVLOPMENT MAKES YOU MORE ACCOUNTABLE TO

FOLLOWING THROUGH TO THE END RATHER THAN TYPED NOTES.

BE BEAUTIFUL AND COOL. Using your own hand writing for your action steps holds you more accountable to following through. Your own handwriting is a useful tool to use when you feel other people don't believe in your dreams in quite the same way that you do.

Your own handwriting helps your reach your goals, much more than typing it out.

If you want your goals to be beautiful and cool, use your own handwriting. Your own hand writing helps your goals gain traction. It seems to pull you in the right direction once you start writing things down by hand.

Writing down intentions alongside your goals seems to have an almost magical mystical quality once done. I referred back to my intentions and found I had followed through on them in more ways than one.

Once you have completed a project refer back to your intentions as a way to review your work, and then create some fresh intentions for your next project. Keep pushing your intentions into new horizons; this will improve all of the work you decide to embark on.

Also when you write down your intentions, you end up narrowing down your talents. When you narrow down your talents to the area you are best at, or need to improve on, you create room for brilliance.

Hard work with intelligent intentions is the key.

ENJOY YOUR GIFT

Chapter 33

REFINING AND DEFINING

Seth Godin in Linchpin talks about thrashing at the beginning of a project because it saves time. Thrashing doesn't just save time; it actually helps you generate more ideas.

Refining (my version of thrashing) helps you define your ideas so much more. You become more eloquent and make use of your intelligence perfectly by refining early you also increase your powers of communication.

As I mentioned at the beginning of this book which is a blog at present, I refined my drawing early by doing a lot of research into art history and by getting inside the minds of the Greats, before working on my drawing collection. Refining can also be gaining relevant knowledge and putting it into professional practice.

Sharing can also be a way of refining and defining your intentions. You get feedback and your ideas and work will improve.....

Sharing can move you forward into new horizons.

Sharing refines and defines your creativity and your art, and following the advice in this book from the very beginning will help you on the road to developing your gift.

You can join me on my Facebook page
www.facebook.com/fashionillustrationmagazine

ARTWORK AND SOCIAL MEDIA DETAILS

Contact me via facebook on

www.facebook.com/fashionillustrationmagazine

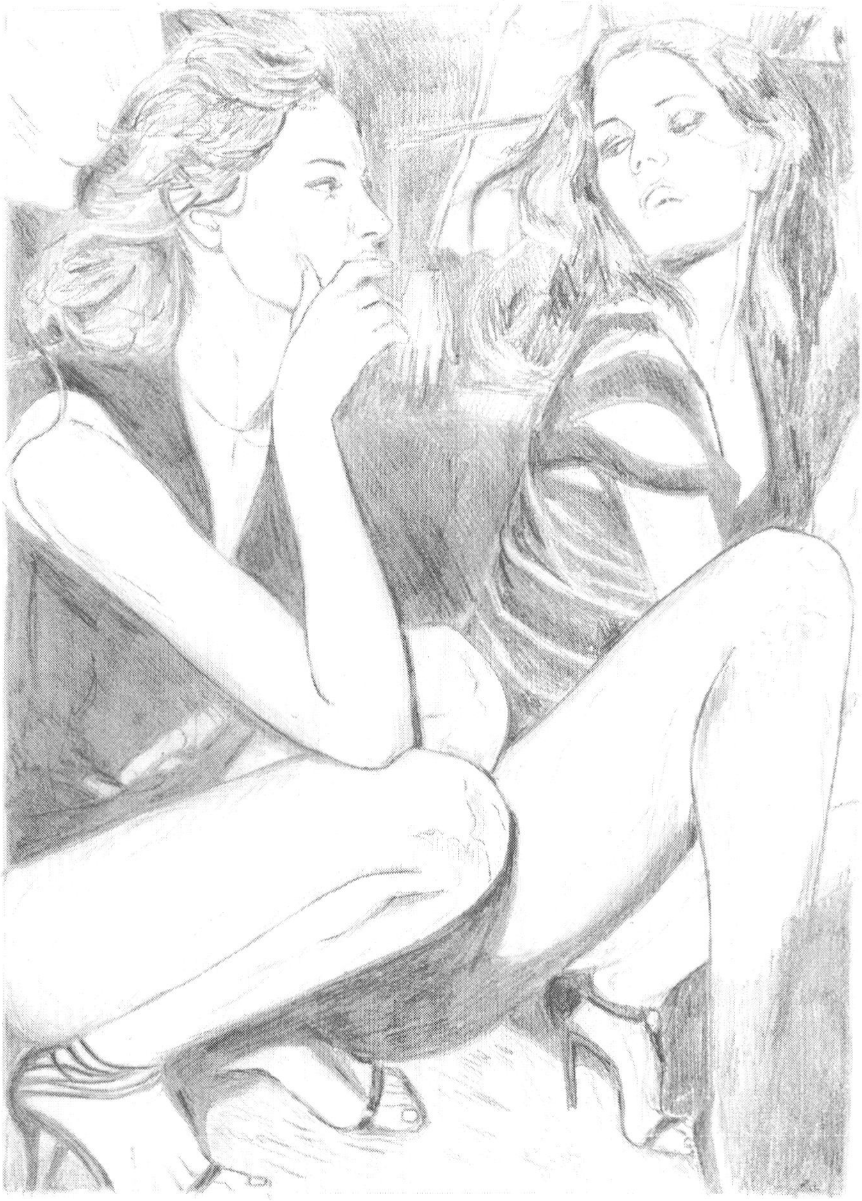

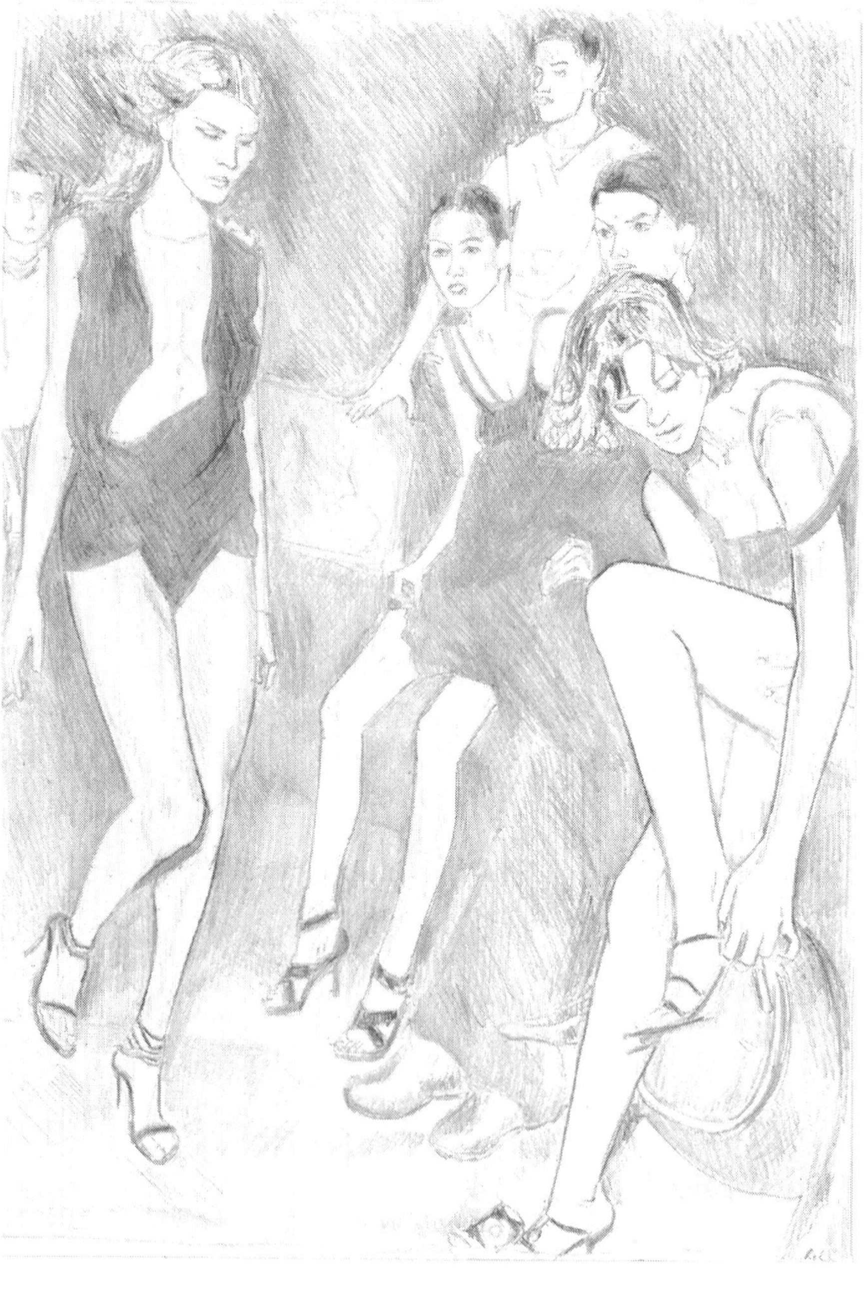

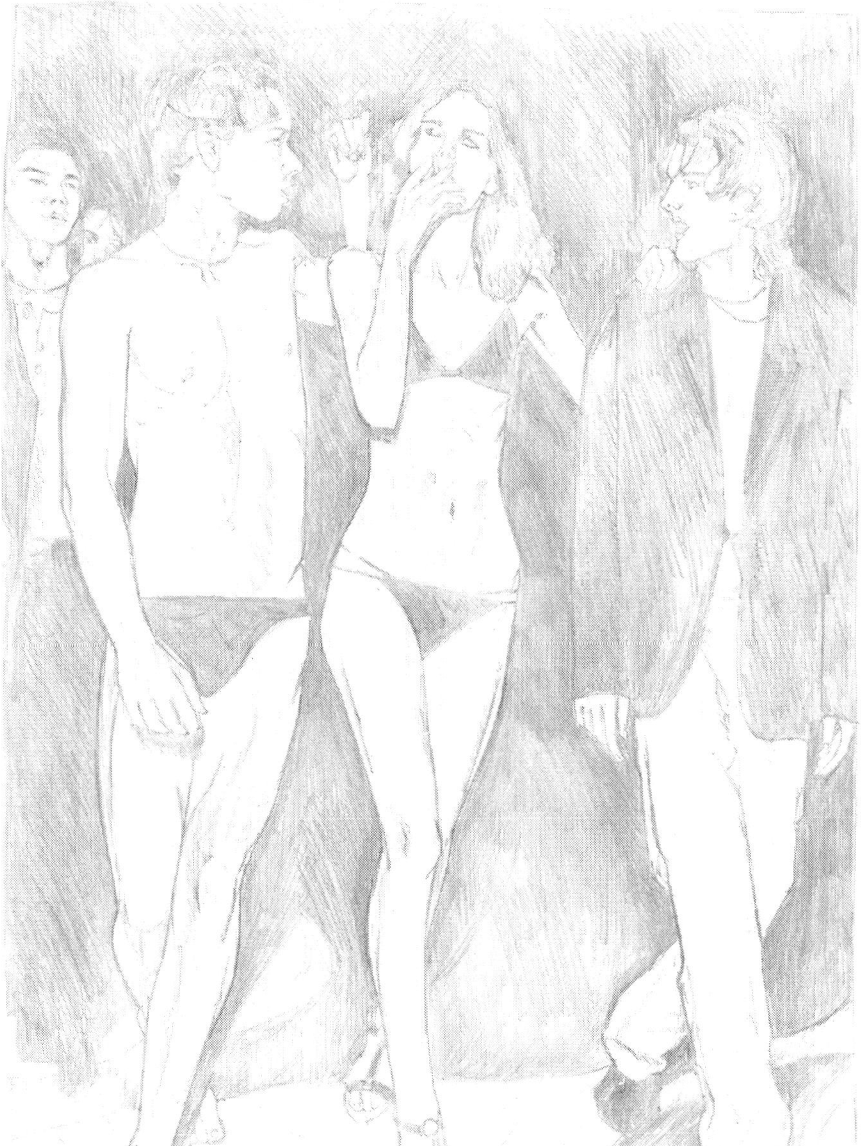

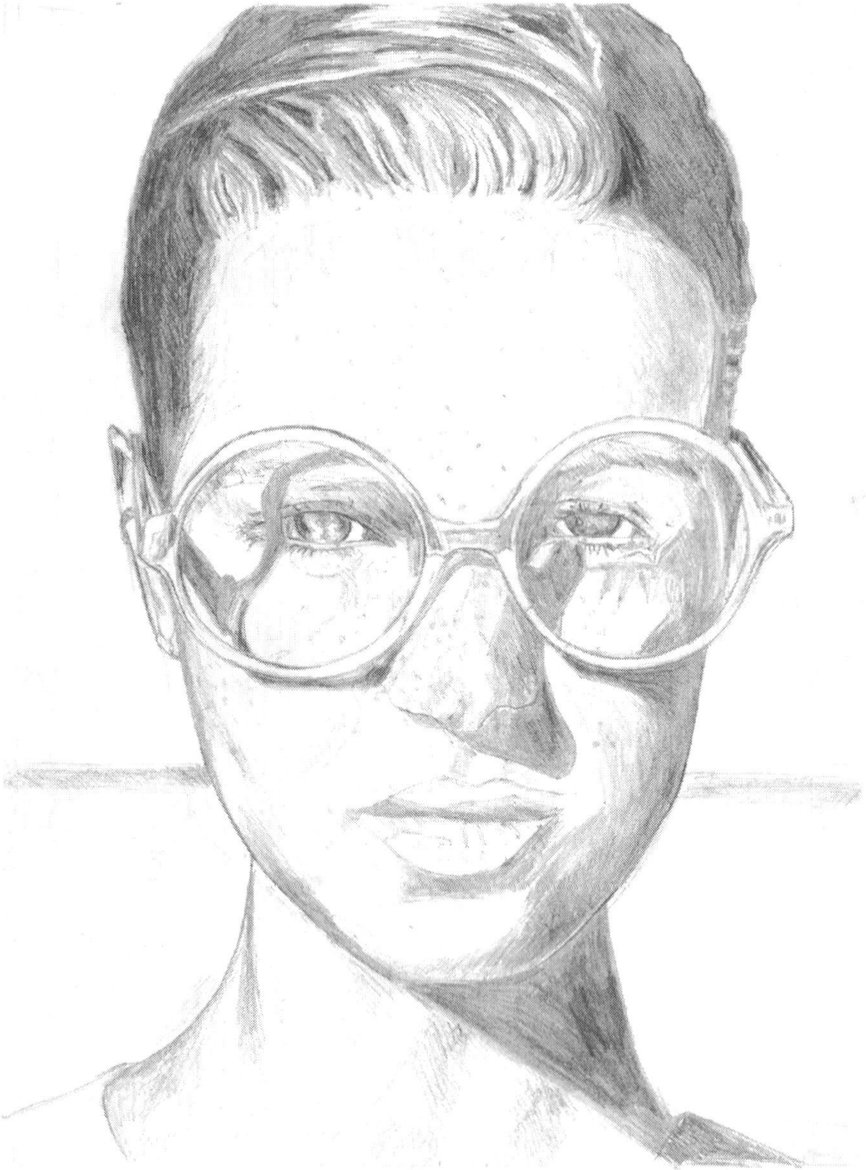

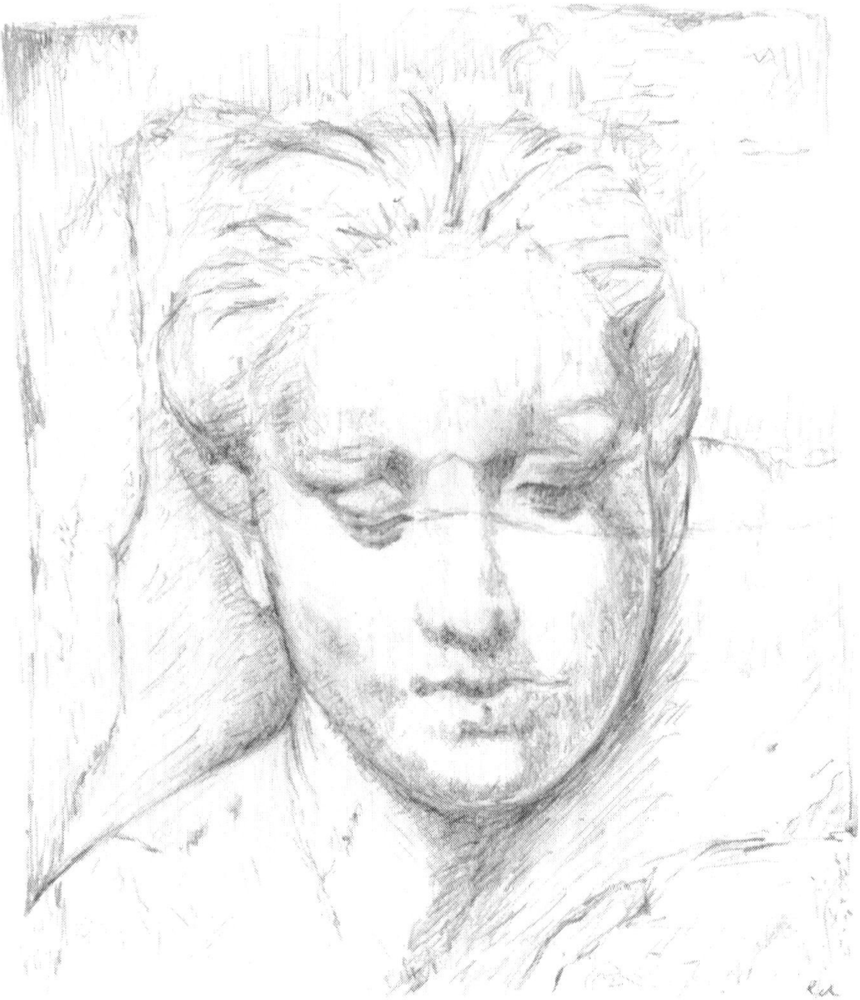

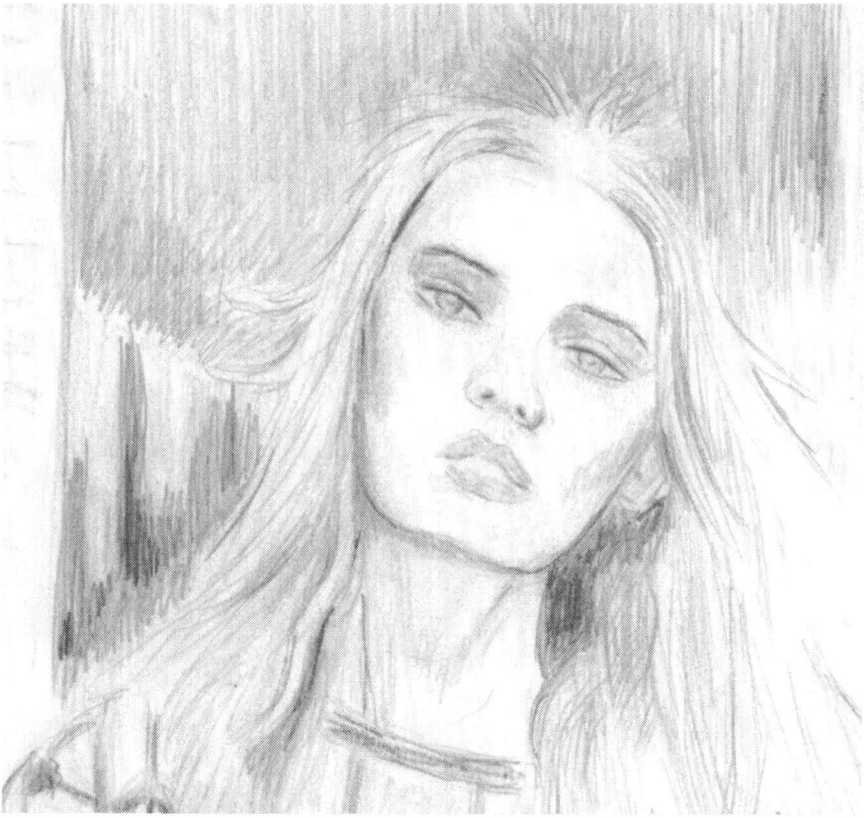

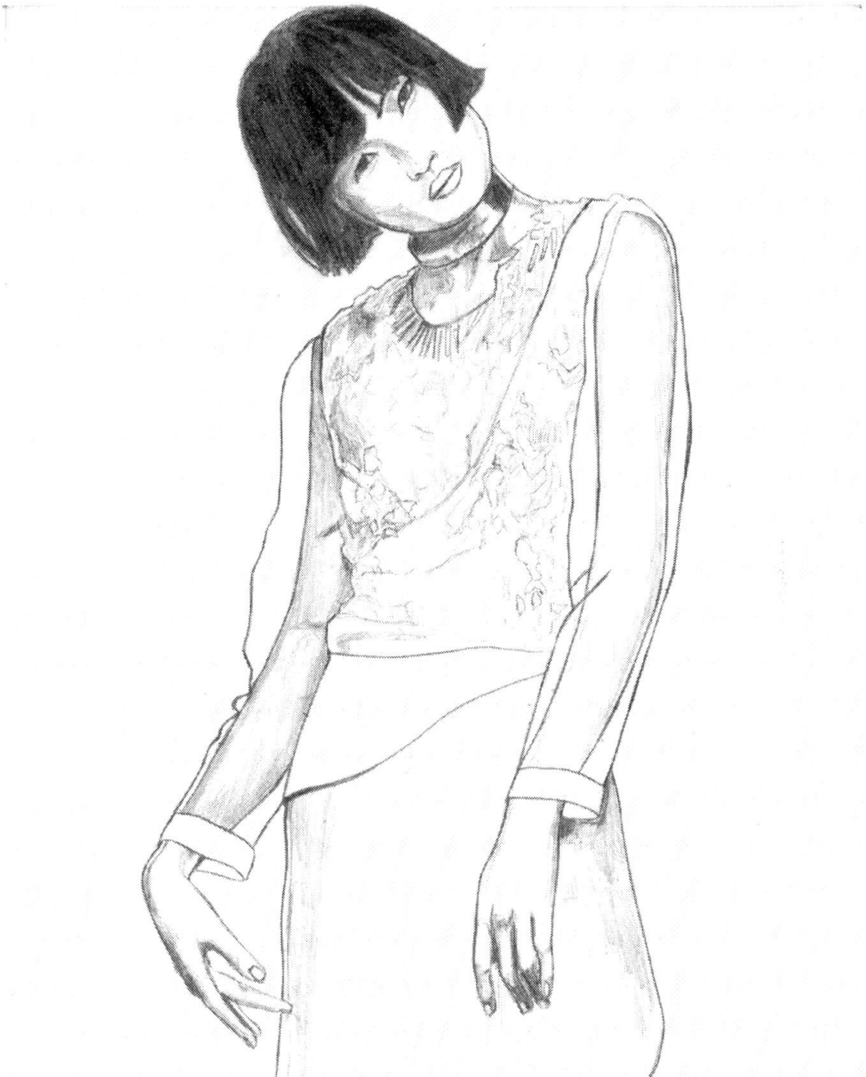

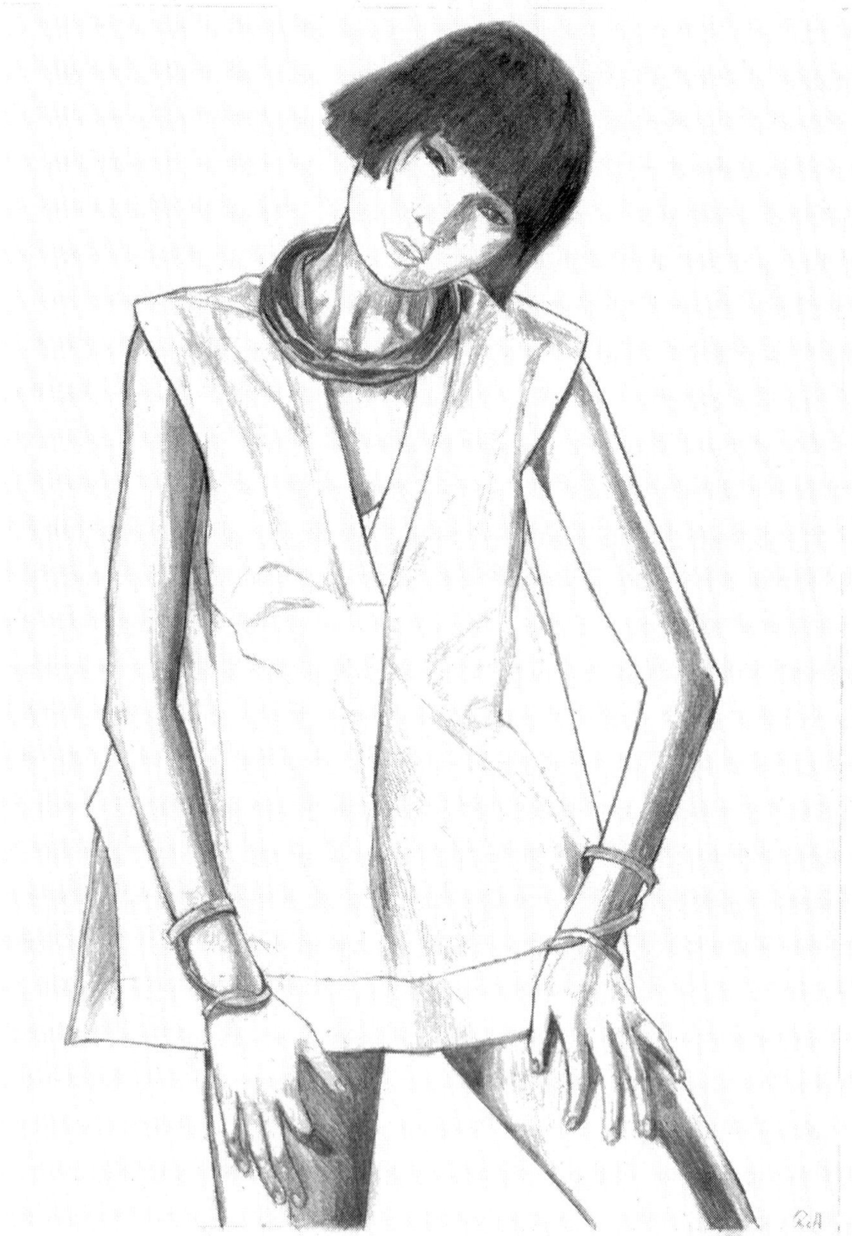

154

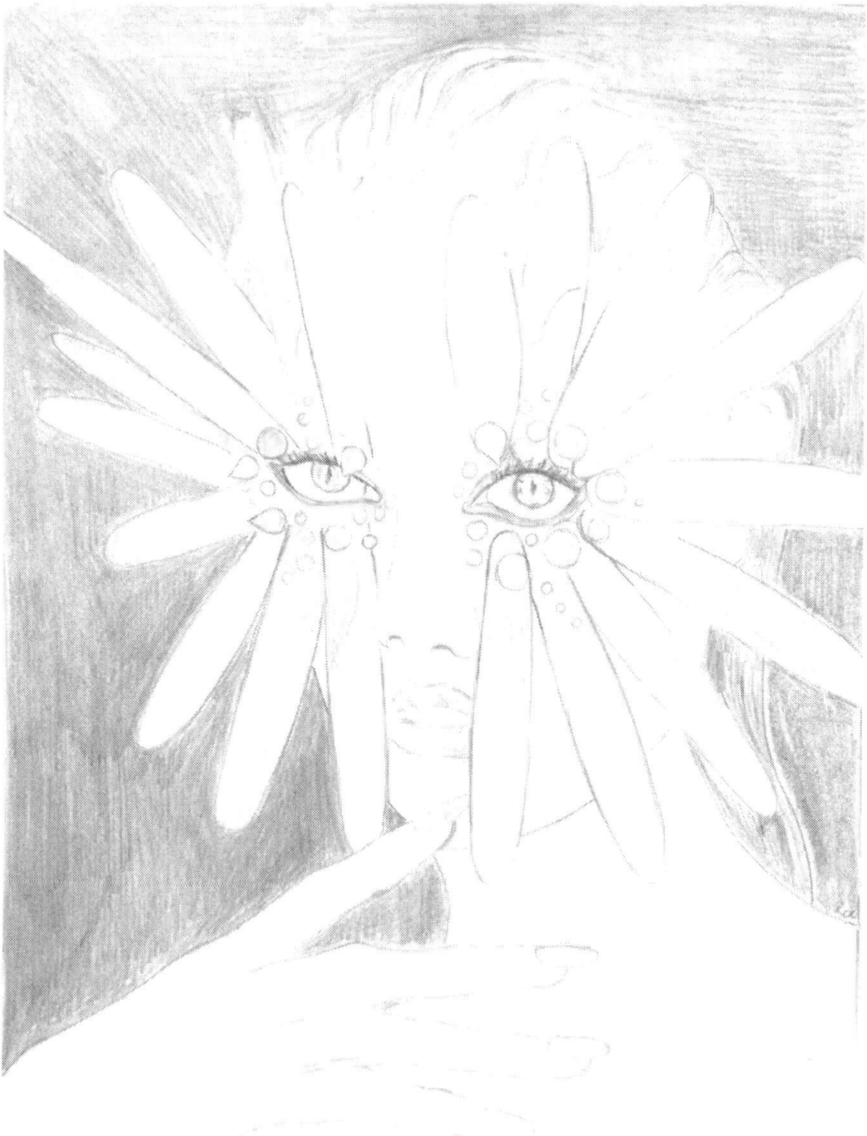

Acknowledgements

These are the books I read that gave me inspiration for this book.

The Magic Of Thinking Big. By David J. Schwartz

Please Don't Do What I Tell, You Do What Needs To Be Done. By Bob Nelson

Making Ideas Happen. By Scot Belsky

The Dip. By Seth Godin

Who Moved My Cheese. By Dr Spencer Johnston

Meatball Sundae. By Seth Godin

Did You Spot The Gorilla. By Richard Wiseman

Get The Life You Really Want. By James Caan

Tribes. By Seth Godin

Ignore Everybody And 39 Other Keys To Creativity. By Hugh Macleod

Linchpin. By Seth Godin

ARTWORK/ILLUSTRATION ACKNOWLEDGEMENTS

The images for the drawings come from various sources.

Elle Magazine

Google Search

Vogue Magazine

Ten Magazine

Commons & Sense

Dazed

Hunger Magazine

Baku Magazine

AnOther Magazine

Full acknowledgements will be given in later editions of this artwork.

Some photos sourced from photographs where source is unknown

THE END

NOTES

NOTES

NOTES

NOTES

NOTES

NOTES

NOTES

NOTES

NOTES

NOTES

Printed in Great Britain
by Amazon.co.uk, Ltd.,
Marston Gate.